TROLLING TRUTHS

FOR TROUT, KOKANEE AND LANDLOCKED KING SALMON

SEP & MARILYN HENDRICKSON

ILLUSTRATIONS BY TOM WATERS

Frank Amato
PORTLAND

ACKNOWLEDGEMENTS

There are many people out there who continue to impact our angling success. We are grateful to our pro staff, our friends and acquaintances...and the believers who read our articles and stories, who use our SEP'S products, and who follow our trolling paths.

A special thank you to Les and Barbara Boyle, without whom SEP'S would never have come into being. In the beginning, they took us fishing...all four of us...in their 12-foot aluminum boat, and showed us how to catch fish in a lake.

Special thanks to those individuals who have supported and helped us from the start: Tony Thiesson, Ed Rice, Bruce

In the beginning...Les and Barbara Boyle.

Wassom, Dan Miller, Tom Malmstadt, Ron and Lynn Gilliss, Bob Smalley, Leo Vrana, Blair Carpender, Richard Burton, Paul Burns, Bill Karr and of course, the dearly departed Larry Green. Tight Lines,

Sep and Marilyn

■ ■ ■ ■ ■ ■ ■ ■ ■ ■ ■ ■ ■ ■ ■

© 2004 Sep and Marilyn Hendrickson

ALL RIGHTS RESERVED. No part of this book may be reproduced or transmitted in any form or by any means, electronic or mechanical, without the written consent of the publisher, except in the case of brief excerpts in critical reviews and articles. All inquiries should be addressed to:

Frank Amato Publications, Inc.

P.O. Box 82112, Portland, Oregon 97282

503.653.8108 • www.amatobooks.com

All photographs by the author unless otherwise noted.

Illustrations: Tom Waters unless otherwise noted

Book & Cover Design: Kathy Johnson

Printed in Singapore

Softbound ISBN: 1-57188-309-6 • UPC: 0-81127-00143-9

1 3 5 7 9 10 8 6 4 2

TABLE OF CONTENTS

■ FOREWORD . . . 4 ■

■ INTRODUCTION . . . 5 ■

■ 1. RIGHT PLACE . . . 6 ■

■ 2. DEPTH AND TEMPERATURE . . . 9 ■

■ 3. "GETTING DOWN" . . . 14 ■

■ 4. DOWNRIGGERS . . . 16 ■

■ 5. DOWNRIGGER DYNAMICS . . . 20 ■

■ 6. NO FISH? . . . 23 ■

■ 7. SIDEPLANERS/HORIZONTAL HUNTING . . . 25 ■

■ 8. VERTICAL HUNTING . . . 28 ■

■ 9. TIME AND DAYS . . . 30 ■

■ 10. TURNOVER TIME . . . 33 ■

■ 11. ALTERNATIVES . . . 35 ■

■ 12. TROLLING SPEED . . . 37 ■

■ 13. LINE AND LEADER . . . 40 ■

■ 14. VIBRATIONS AND ATTRACTORS . . . 44 ■

■ 15. LURES...COLORS . . . 48 ■

■ 16. COMMON SENSE ON SCENTS . . . 51 ■

■ 17. TROLLING FLIES . . . 53 ■

■ 18. TROLLING GRUBS . . . 55 ■

■ 19. HOOK SET . . . 56 ■

■ 20. RODS AND REELS . . . 57 ■

■ 21. RAINBOW TROUT . . . 60 ■

■ 22. CUTTHROAT TROUT . . . 61 ■

■ 23. BROWN TROUT . . . 62 ■

■ 24. KOKANEE SALMON . . . 64 ■

■ 25. LANDLOCKED KING SALMON. . . 65 ■

■ 26. MACKINAW . . . 66 ■

■ 27. STATE-OF-THE-ART TECHNOLOGY. . . 67 ■

■ 28. GET A CLUE! . . . 71 ■

■ 29. SEP'S ON THE INTERNET AND RADIO . . . 78 ■

■ IN CLOSING . . . 79 ■

FOREWORD

"It's all in the presentation"
... whoever said it first, must have been an angler.

If you take your angling as seriously as we do...we believe these are interesting and informative guidelines that will change the way you fish...for the better! If you enjoy catching rainbow trout, German browns, cutthroat, char, mackinaw, brook trout, landlocked kokanee and king salmon in coldwater lakes...come along with us!

We share tactics, techniques and the how-tos we have experienced that will increase your success rate. We share what we have learned in our personal travels and angling adventures plus information gleaned from experts throughout the country.

This book is about freshwater trolling...the ultralight way.

Anglers have trolled for years, using any and all systems, and they have been successful...some more so than others. Trolling for fish is not rocket science but doing it well is properly utilizing the new and innovative techniques and technology available. The way we do it is a little different!

We like it LIGHT...ULTRALIGHT. Our equipment is light – our rods, reels, line and lures. We like to use attractors that create very little resistance, that have little or no drag. In short, we want to "feel the fight"...each run, headshake and tug of the fish, to enjoy the opportunity by maximizing the fight.

This book shares a great deal of our own expertise and experiences...but we surely do not profess to know it all. As a matter of fact, we are quick to admit we continue to learn more every time we go fishing, and so should you.

Our own knowledge and experience developed as technology and electronics began to make a strong impact on fishing and the average angler. We have certainly been in on the cutting edge and what a trip this has been! We fondly refer to our lives as the "big bubble" and our friends and acquaintances know how thankful we are to be able to do what we enjoy most.

We fish like you do. Some days are good, some great, and still others leave us wondering what could have been done differently. We are not experts, we're "experienced", and simply happen to go fishing more than most folks.

We willingly share what we have learned so far. Our goal is to present hard facts to make your fishing adventures more productive and enjoyable. The rest will be up to you.

INTRODUCTION

"The difference between a boat ride and fishing...is catching fish"

Primarily we troll. This offers the opportunity to cover more water or surface acres, thereby increasing the chances of locating more fish. It allows for the presentation of lures or bait right in the face of the fish! It also provides a more natural presentation. Now, don't get this wrong...each year, monster fish are caught by bait dunkers, too. They catch their fair share of trophies, but trollers enjoy the challenge of unlocking the combination for hook-ups, using experience, judgment and a wide variety of ultralight equipment.

The Sep's Trolling Machine.

Trolling can be as simple as letting line and lure out behind the boat, or as complex as a melding of electronics, technology, experience and techniques.

Trolling involves idling the boat across the surface of the lake while placing offerings in the **right place**, at the **right time**, at the **right depth**, at the **right speed**, with the **right lure**, in the **right color**, with the **right action**, and **proper presentation**. Sounds easy, doesn't it!

Angling success is not measured by doing most things right, but by doing everything right.

It is that mix of past experience, consistency of presentation plus knowledge, that routinely brings an angler great days of fishing. A myriad of high-tech electronics, such as global positioning systems, auto pilot steering, sonar locators, sidefinders, electronic downriggers, underwater cameras and more, are available to assist in catching more fish, but be assured, anglers can find enhanced success by simply concentrating on the often overlooked BASICS of freshwater trolling.

1. RIGHT PLACE

"It is as important to know where to fish as how to fish."

First and foremost, an angler must be able to find the fish! This takes some thought and a little common sense. Every lake or reservoir has certain physical characteristics that attract fish. When an angler knows where and what to look for, the chances of catching fish increase dramatically. Anglers should do their homework, starting by checking out key areas on a good-quality map.

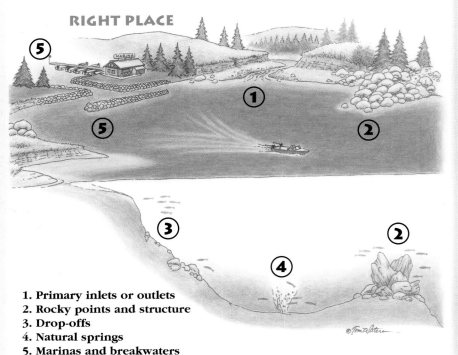

RIGHT PLACE

1. Primary inlets or outlets
2. Rocky points and structure
3. Drop-offs
4. Natural springs
5. Marinas and breakwaters

Primary Inlets and Outlets

One of the prime locations for trolling in a lake is within 100 to 200 yards of primary inlets and outlets. The cool, fresh waters of rivers, creeks and streams flow through the lake, bringing highly-oxygenated water and a broad spectrum of forage for trout and salmon to feed upon. Insects, aquatic life, minnows and small trout and salmon fry are but a few of the natural baits drawn downstream to a lake through its tributaries. Feeder streams, like primary inlets, and natural currents following old river beds throughout lakes, will bring abundant sources of food to the feeding fish waiting around these areas.

Dams, at the exit of lakes, act as primary outlets and the face of any dam will often provide large accumulations of fish. Natural currents bring forage such as disoriented baitfish to the spillway and fish will definitely gather there. The area where a lake empties into a river or creek will certainly hold fish, waiting for an easy meal. Insects and other food sources float or drift on the surface or in the current toward the outlet. Large trout often hang out near outlets, slurping up anything edible floating past.

Rocky Points and Structure

These provide natural holding and feeding areas. Submerged islands, trees, old dams, bridges, brush piles and other structures all provide protection and are productive locations. The shape and structure of a lake and its points create natural pathways for fish. An enriched food chain is created in these rocky areas as aquatic life such as freshwater shrimp, leeches, emergers and minnows move among the rocks to feed on plankton and other forage. The organisms growing on and around rocky areas attract baitfish, which attract smaller game fish, which in turn attract larger game fish…and so on.

Drop-offs

Trout definitely like milling around the edges of drop-offs. They know that minnows hide and cruise in these areas, feeding and trying not to be fed upon, plus drop-offs offer them easy escape routes to deeper waters. Trollers working around drop-offs can often enjoy excellent action.

Natural Springs

Natural springs are found in many lakes, particularly in the volcanic regions of the West. These underwater springs bring a nearly continuous supply of fresh, highly-oxygenated water into the lake. In many cases, this water is warmer, or cooler, than that of the lake, and this often attracts huge schools of baitfish to these ideal condition areas. At times, the baitfish drawn to these locations can be so thick, they will signal a false bottom reading on a fish locator. Trout, kokanee and landlocked king salmon hang near these natural feeding grounds.

Marinas and Breakwaters

Just like in rocky areas, a food chain is established around marinas, boat docks and the rocks of breakwaters. Think about it, how many times have you seen huge schools of minnows around the pilings of a marina? Or, have you heard about or seen, big fish lurking under docks? Yes, there are definitely game fish around, trying for a quick and easy meal!

Research

Knowing where to find fish is half the battle in becoming a successful troller and doing research before heading out to an unfamiliar location will pay off. Carefully examine maps of the lake, looking for areas that may hold or support game fish. Check fishing newspapers and ask questions of local tackle shop and marina operators. They want you to catch fish, spread the word and return.

The Internet offers satellite views, topo maps and vast amounts of information on websites, in chat rooms and from state and federal agencies.

Often the quickest way to learn about a new body of water is to book an experienced, professional fishing guide. It is possible to learn in one day of fishing with a knowledgeable guide, as much as you would learn in several years on your own. If the guide is a quality guide—check referrals before booking—he will openly share tackle, baits, techniques, tactics and locations that will produce fish. The information you glean can save many hours of frustrating trolling time. After "picking" the guide's brain, you can easily apply the learned techniques when you head out on your own. The cost of a guide becomes minimal when compared to the time, expense and effort it would take to do it on your own.

Another Tip

When wondering where to go on a lake, look for other boats. They will dot most every productive locale. If you have doubts about where to fish or how deep, don't hesitate to ask questions of passing anglers as they are generally a friendly bunch.

Another possibility, troll the same path the others are fishing. General courtesy dictates that you should not troll too closely to another boater and it is a good idea to keep at least a 30- to 50-yard buffer zone to avoid crossing over or tangling lines with fellow anglers. Valuable fish-catching time can be wasted while untangling lines or downriggers because of trolling too close to another boat or trolled offerings. It also makes the errant troller an unpopular member of the group, putting it mildly!

2. DEPTH AND TEMPERATURE

"One of the most common mistakes made is presenting terminal offerings at the wrong depth."

Preciseness of presentation is key to angling success. Anglers often think they are trolling at the right depth, but can actually be off by a significant distance. It is important to troll offerings within the strike or attack range of the quarry.

TEMPERATURE LAYERS

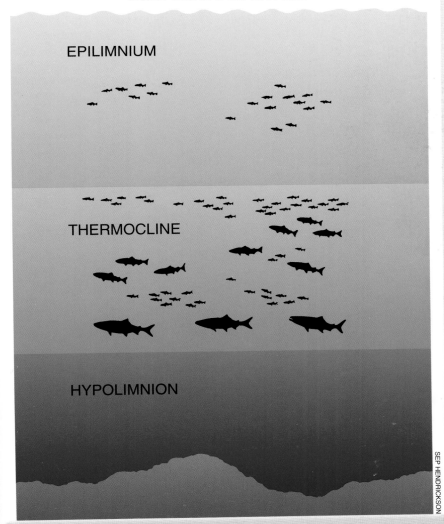

EPILIMNIUM

THERMOCLINE

HYPOLIMNION

SEP HENDRICKSON

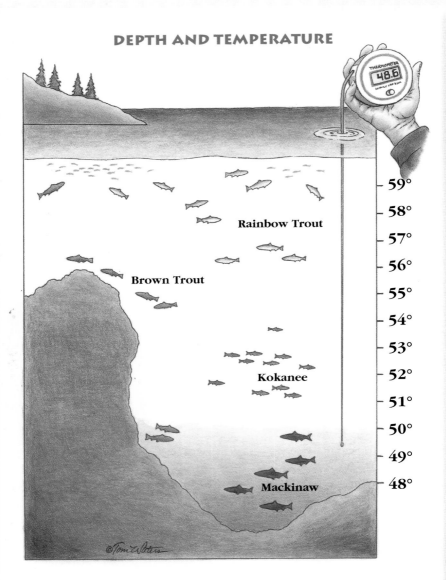

Fish are cold-blooded. Their body temperature is the same as the surrounding water and every species of trout and salmon has a preferred temperature. Whenever this ideal temperature water is available to them, fish spend as much time as possible at that level. Trout and salmon species thrive in water, rich in oxygen in the 52- to 58-degree range. This area, regardless of its depth, is known as the "thermocline". This is the area where fish will be most active and where they will be more willing to expend the energy required to chase and strike a lure or bait.

Before attempting to intercept fish roaming below the surface, it is important to have a simple understanding of the make up of the lake.

The upper layer of the lake is known as the "epilimnium". This layer contains an assortment of forage for trout and salmon, such as minnows, baitfish and aquatic insect life. The temperature and oxygen content of the epilimnium varies greatly, depending upon the season.

Immediately after ice out, the surface and shallow water along the shoreline attracts fish searching for the first waters to be warmed by the rays of the sun. In the summer, the epilimnium is often warm, uncomfortable and too low in oxygen content for cold water species. Fish may venture into these

Tom Coster found the right temperature zone to intercept this 6-pound rainbow.

warmer than preferred waters, especially in the early morning and late evening hours but normally they do not stay long. They prefer to live in the deeper, cooler waters of the lake's mid-range, known as the "thermocline". In the fall and early winter, weather and wind changes cause the surface and shallows to cool and become oxygenated, bringing game fish to the epilimnium layer of the lake, once again.

The thermocline is the nutrient and oxygen rich water of ideal temperature that is the summer home of coldwater species. For the most part, trout and salmon find themselves living in this concentrated ideal band of water. This band of perfect water temperature and habitat is exactly where lures or bait need to be.

The lower level of the lake is known as the "hypolimnium". It is poor in oxygen and food supplies and offers little attraction to the fish. To put it simply ... it is a DEAD zone.

California Department of Fish & Game associate Fisheries Biologist Paul Chappell carefully examines rainbow trout caught 23-30 feet deep, in the thermocline.

Preferred Temperature Ranges

Rainbow Trout	52-58 degrees
Brown and Brook Trout	50-60 degrees
Mackinaw or Lake Trout	40-52 degrees
King Salmon	52-54 degrees
Kokanee Salmon	52-56 degrees

How to Find the Thermocline

One of the most important pieces of equipment an angler should have in the tackle box, and one that very few have, is a water temperature thermometer. If used methodically and properly, a thermometer can provide information about proper trolling depth, and what color and type of lure to use. By testing and locating the upper and lower limits of the thermocline, an angler can find the exact depths to present offerings, whether trolling or stillfishing.

A wide variety of thermometers are available, ranging in cost, depending on how fancy an angler wants to get. Available for around $10, a tube thermometer can be attached and lowered on fishing line. For about $50, a digital gauge with cable and probe gives L.E.D. readouts on a small hand-held screen. Or, the zealous angler can go all the way and purchase a temperature sensing unit…on a dash-mounted screen, a digital readout of the temperature and speed at the downrigger ball is available…truly state-of-the-art electronics!

Watch the screen of the fish locator closely and make note of the depths at which fish are visible. Many high quality fish locators on the market today provide clear pictures of what anglers are traveling over and can identify the proximity of the thermocline by indicating depths where fish are holding. It is important to learn to interpret and believe what the fish locator shows. Periodically re-check your manual to re-familiarize yourself with the basics of its operation.

The thermocline can generally be identified with the use of high quality locators by turning the sensitivity to maximum, then locating the colder denser water. The thermocline does not run at the same depths throughout the lake. Note the levels where fish are holding, then present the offerings within that range. By carefully watching the screen of the locator and adjusting depths as necessary, an angler can intercept the thermocline and greater numbers of cruising fish. For the most part, fish will be in the thermocline, but there are times they do travel in and out of the band with frequency, especially when feeding heavily. Take the lake's temperature when traveling about to ensure that offerings are placed within or close to water of the ideal temperature range.

Knowing the temperature at the depth where lures or bait are placed is definitely information an angler needs to know.

DEPTH AND TEMPERATURE

3. "GETTING DOWN"

"There are a variety of ways of getting down to the thermocline."

Adding lead weights, leaded keels or banana weights will certainly help get lures or baits down, but how far down do they go? The addition of weight is only guesswork at best and it comes between you and the fish. Even if a fish or two is caught, the troller is never really sure the correct depth has been reached and most likely the action would have been much better if the lure or bait had been precisely in the thermocline.

There are many charts and guidelines to help anglers determine actual depth when trolling with weights. The relationship between speed of the boat, lure weight, lure drag and action, weight of line, length of leader line, wind and current direction will determine where or at what depth terminal offerings will run. There are far too many variables for an angler to accurately predict the true running depth of the lure.

Diving planes will take terminal offerings down…but just how accurate are they? Each such device has it's own formula for line diameter and depth and it does get down…but to what depth? Keep the instructions that come with the original set-up as the many variables necessitate regular consultation! Diving devices do require the use of heavier tackle as they create an added strain on the rod, reel and line, which certainly interferes with the enjoyment of the fight.

For controlled depth fishing the only answer is state-of-the-art downriggers.

Trolling the depths, ready for action.

Lead-core line revolutionized trolling many years ago. Each thirty-foot section of line is a different color and a good rule of thumb, or guess, is for every color out, the line drops about five feet, if trolling one mph. Knowing the correct trolling speed is essential for accuracy and some varieties of line are designed to drop even deeper than the "five-feet-per color" standard. To intercept fish in a 40-foot thermocline, let out eight colors, placing the lure 240 feet behind the boat! This line is big and bulky and requires specialized tackle to handle the weight and size. Ask yourself, how deep does my lead-core line really drop? How fast am I trolling? Once again, guesswork at best.

The end result? To be able to catch more fish, get down with accuracy, down to the depth needed to intercept more fish! To ensure proper depth control and to eliminate guesswork, there is only one solution—use down-riggers!

4. DOWNRIGGERS

"If you want to get down accurately, you definitely need a downrigger."

Downriggers are state-of-the-art in controlled depth fishing. To an angler, they can be the "secret to success" or a "nightmare of frustration". Downriggers, suitable to your needs, combined with a high quality fish locator, provide a distinct advantage.

The most common mistake made when trolling is having terminal offerings at an unknown or incorrect depth. Some anglers simply hit the water and let out lines. Some run lines on top, others end up scattering lines at varying depths. A myriad of devices are used to help get down, but just how deep is the lure, really? It is extremely important to know exactly how deep terminal tackle is running...fish can only look up; therefore your terminal offerings must stay above the fish.

When summer temperatures warm our lakes, trout and salmon move to deeper waters in search of the thermocline and forage. Anglers using lead-core line, diving planes or heavy sinkers to get down, find these methods to be an inexact science at best. These techniques require the use of much heavier rods, reels, and line...resulting in far less enjoyable experiences when fish are caught.

Without a doubt, the single most effective way to get lures or bait accurately to the proper depth is to use downriggers. This method allows trollers to fish deep with light tackle and, most importantly, to enjoy the sport of fighting the fish. Too often, heavier tackle means "winching" in your fish, thereby not enjoying the fight. TO FEEL THE FIGHT...USE ULTRA-LIGHT.

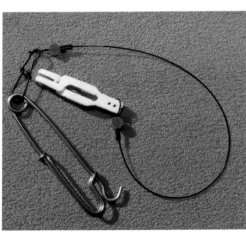

Sep's Sure Release—reliable, small one-hand operation, plus Sure Stacker.

A downrigger is simply a reel-type device that takes line and lure down into the water with accuracy and efficiency. The downrigger ball, or weight, is secured to the downrigger cable, to which a line release is attached. This takes fishing line and lure down to the desired depth.

FINDING THE RIGHT DEPTH

When a fish hooks up, the line is pulled free of the release, leaving the angler to fight the fish with no resistance.

At one time, downriggers were out of the price range of many anglers, but that is certainly not the case any longer. They were originally used in saltwater and heavy fresh water applications, but current models are definitely practical for light line use. Manufacturers now make downriggers of high quality that will fit any budget, with prices that range from fifty to $1,000 each. There are even downriggers practical and efficient enough to bring along to clamp on rental boats, if desired.

The troller has many choices; from simple-to-operate hand-crank units to electronic computerized wonders that track the bottom of the lake and automatically raise and lower offerings. Or, an ingenious angler can simply take a length of rope or heavy line, mark off five foot increments, attach a downrigger ball and release, clip on the fishing line and lower the basic unit over the side of the boat by hand. This "poor man's downrigger" works and it costs less than $15!

The size or weight of the downrigger ball can vary, depending upon the application and the downrigger. Keep it light, and generally a six-pound ball is plenty for trout and kokanee angling. When trolling slowly, water resistance is a concern and using a heavy ball is not necessary. When trolling in deep water or at faster speeds, a heavier, eight- or ten-pound ball works best, assuming the downrigger can hold such weight. The objective here is to maintain accurate depth control by keeping the downrigger ball as straight down as possible, minimizing "blow-back" caused by drag in the water. The more cable that is out and the deeper the lure is, the greater the drag and blow-back.

When trolling with a downrigger, we recommend not holding the rod, but rather, placing it firmly in the rod holder, then "loading" it by tightening up line until the rod forms a graceful arc. When a fish hits and pops the line free from the release, the loaded up rod will take up slack line and semi-set the hook.

Proper use of downriggers is essential to angling success. We consider downriggers to be absolute necessities and use them, as various situations warrant, from the surface to the lake's bottom. We generally run four Cannon DT-20 electric downriggers on our Design Concepts, two out the side and two off the stern.

Some seasoned anglers have enhanced the use of downriggers by adding a "dropper line" utilized for trolling two depths at the same time, on one fishing rod. This method consists of attaching a swivel to one end of a five-foot leader and a light-weight lure to the oth-er. After the main line

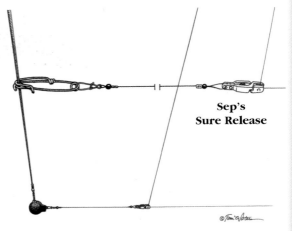

Sep's
Sure Release

is connected to the downrigger release and set at the desired depth, the swivel on the five-foot leader is attached (to the main line) and the lure end is tossed into the water toward the back of the boat.

As the angler trolls along, the lure will slowly sink below the surface and move to a point approximately half-way down—the apex of the bow in the line—to the downrigger ball. For example, if the downrigger is set at forty feet deep, the dropper line will run near twenty feet, allowing the angler to attract more fish by covering two depths. If the only fish being caught are on the dropper line, then the downrigger is set too deep. Raise it up and try again, you might catch fish on both lines at the same time!

This technique is very effective and can be used on any waters where downriggers are used. One thing that can frustrate the angler is the dropper line tangling with the main line when bringing in a fish. If this happens, simply cut the leader at the swivel, or lure, and pull it out. If another dropper line is tied and ready to go, the angler loses no fishing time. The effectiveness of this technique quickly becomes obvious...it is easy to master and will certainly improve chances of catching fish.

Sure Release connected to line, prior to dropping downrigger down.

The choice of a suitable "downrigger release" is also important. Many accessories of this type were originally geared for heavier applications and were difficult to attach, adjust and utilize.

SEP'S Sure Release addresses the specific needs of ultralight anglers. It is small enough to handle light line needs easily and is designed to dependably and smoothly release on the strike of a small to medium weight fish. The release can also be tripped with just a flip of the rod tip. Because of its simple "pinch" design, line can be easily and quickly inserted. The spring inside can be adjusted forward or backward to get a heavier or lighter release of line on the strike. The firm setting can be utilized when using a heavier line or when the angler wants to control the release of the line.

The release has a wire leader with a snap for connecting it directly to the downrigger cable, or to the downrigger weight itself. Also available is the Super Lines release with a firmer grip for the new ultra-small diameters of super lines.

SEP'S Sure Stacker is a "companion" device, to be used with a downrigger. This small metal clip allows the angler to troll two lines on one downrigger cable. Stackers make it possible to fish two different depths off the same downrigger. Simply put out the first line as usual, attach the Sure Stacker to the downrigger cable then attach the second line and send it all down.

DOWNRIGGERS

5. DOWNRIGGER DYNAMICS

"The importance of accurate depth control cannot be overstressed."

Imagine the fish locator indicating several schools of nice-sized fish, holding suspended at the 40-foot mark, in 80 feet of water. You're trolling at a speed of one-half to one mile per hour, pulling a standard rigged flasher and lure. You have just let out line...the flasher rig is 100 feet behind the boat. You know fish are holding at 40 feet and quickly lower your offering. How deep would you lower it to intercept fish cruising at 40 feet? 40 feet...right? WRONG!

Here's the hitch! Allow for the natural drop of the terminal rig! Trolling flashers or dodgers, 100 feet behind the boat, at one mph., can cause the terminal rig to drop as much as ten percent...from five to ten feet, depending upon trolling speed and size of flashers and lures being used.

By lowering the downrigger to 25 feet, the terminal flasher rig will be running at or near, 35 feet. This is five feet above the fish...within perfect attack range. Often trollers fail to take this into account and end up with offerings well below the fish, subsequently striking out, time after time.

This is the SINGLE, BIGGEST mistake that anglers make.

Anglers must know exactly how deep lures and bait are in relation to the fish. It is critical to keep offerings above fish, preferably within a comfortable strike range of three to five feet. The eyes of fish are located near the top of their heads, enabling them to see silhouettes of bait upward, against the light surface. It is much better to have the lure or bait as much as twenty feet above the fish, rather than one foot below. Fish DO NOT look down!

Trout are likely to be spooked by downrigger weights and wire. They will move away from intimidating boat noise and approaching downrigger balls as the boat passes nearby or overhead. If "short-lining", that is, running a lure a short distance behind the boat, chances are you will pass by targeted fish and rarely have a hit. Think about it...you are using a six pound, or larger, downrigger ball. When this comes through or past a school of fish, they will definitely move off to the side. If the lure is right behind the downrigger ball, within ten feet or so, the spread out fish will miss the offering.

If you are after bigger, smarter, more wary trout, drop the offering back...way back. Greater success is found by disassociating terminal offerings, lures or bait, from the boat and engine noise. This can be done easily by keeping lures at least 100 feet behind the downrigger ball. The fish may still move out of the way of the ball, but will have adequate time to return to its original spot and may pursue the offering, once the weight has passed by. At some lakes, fish are so finicky that a troller may need to let out 200

DOWNRIGGING

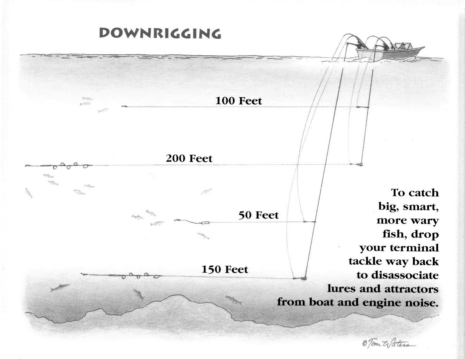

100 Feet

200 Feet

50 Feet

150 Feet

To catch big, smart, more wary fish, drop your terminal tackle way back to disassociate lures and attractors from boat and engine noise.

©Tom Waters

feet or more of line, to fool big, elusive trout. Remember…allow for the natural drop of terminal tackle.

There are times to down-rig deep and times to down-rig shallow. Cold weather and ideal water temperatures bring hungry trout to the surface to feed on minnows, baitfish and other insect and aquatic life that venture into the surface waters or shallow shorelines. Sub-freezing temperatures will cause moss and grasses to die and float to the surface, making top-lining tactics difficult and ineffective when weeds get picked up by lines every few minutes. To reduce the out-of-water, down-time action caused by having to clean lines, try this…using the downrigger, lower offerings to just below the surface at two to five feet. This tactic allows lures or bait to stay shallow, where the fish are, and the troller can continue top-line action without the constant interruption of clearing weeds from the line and terminal offerings.

Schooling fish, such as kokanee and landlocked king salmon, present a different scenario. These species are highly competitive for food sources and are not readily spooked by downrigger balls and cables. They will follow, pursue and strike offerings as close as three feet from the downrigger ball. When a school is located or a fish hooks up, it is a good idea to run tight turns back through the same area, staying in touch with the school. Short-lining ten to twenty feet behind the downrigger ball, enables anglers to "turn on a dime" and pass quickly back through the same school of fish,

To catch big smart, more wary fish, drop terminal tackle way back and disassociate lures and attractors from boat and engine noise.

rather than making the wide sweeping turn of a "long-liner". Keep a close eye on the fish locator as schools of salmon may be found at different levels around the lake. Just because they are caught at 40 feet in one spot, does not mean the next school will be at that same depth.

Early-season kokanee or king salmon are found scattered about the lake with very little schooling activity and even though they do not easily spook with short lines, it is recommended that anglers long-line off the downrigger to best intercept these fish. Trolling with 75 to 100 feet of line behind the downrigger provides adequate time to make necessary depth adjustments for each scattered fish spotted on the locator. When passing over fish, adjust trolled offerings precisely, keeping lures or bait five feet above the fish. This method increases the odds of success by ensuring that as many scattered fish as possible get to see the trolled offerings.

As the season progresses into summer, salmon will be found in small schools of just a few fish at a time. By early fall, and before the spawn, salmon are found in schools of hundreds and often thousands of fish at a time. This is when the short-line, tight-turn technique really produces.

A kokanee bite is anything but consistent! One day it is wide open, the next day the bite is off...big time! The locator screen can light up, indicating an abundance of fish and the depth at which they are holding, but getting a hit is always a challenge. The kokanee bite can start and stop, all day long. Periods of peak activity can be followed by lulls of up to an hour or more and then it's wide-open action again. Don't give up too early, stick with it!

Trolling, stillfishing, casting lures or fly fishing...the importance of accurate depth control and presentation cannot be overstressed.

6. NO FISH?

"Just because you can't see them, doesn't mean they aren't there."

Sometimes, no matter where you troll, the locator simply shows "no fish"! You would swear you were fishing in the Dead Sea! So you try deeper water, shallower water, opposite end of the lake...still nothing! Don't give up, you may be in for the treat of your life.

This is a fairly common occurrence at higher-elevation lakes during early season, cold water angling, especially in those lakes with shallow water and/or gradual tapering shore- lines. Until lakes begin to stratify and the thermocline of ideal temperature develops, fish will

Bottomline has incorporated side finding technology into fish locators.

continue to prowl the shallows, the shoreline and the surface, with only occasional trips to deeper waters in search of food supplies.

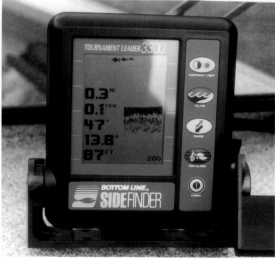

Just because they are not visible on the locator, doesn't mean they are not there...fish can certainly be very close by. If fish are holding in shallow water or just below the surface in deeper water, they will rarely be seen on the locator, no matter how sensitive it is. As the boat approaches, fish spook and tend to move out to the side and scatter. This obviously places them outside the very limited range of the sonar signals of the locator. The cone- shaped signal from the locator is a visual image of a very small area beneath the boat. It might look like there are no fish, but they can definitely be there for the taking, if the troller can get the offering out to the side to intercept them.

Computrol, manufacturer of Bottomline electronic locators, has developed SIDEFINDER technology. This unique improvement in sonar systems allows the angler to see not only down, but up to 240 feet directly to each side of the boat. It detects fish holding or moving off to the side as the angler trolls along.

A device called the SIDEPLANER can certainly assist in catching fish that have moved off to the sides. A sideplaner makes it possible for a troller to

Sidefinder technology and sideplaners pay off. Marilyn, holding a 5 1/2-pound rainbow, caught using sideplane technology and sideplaners.

Rainbow trout caught sideplaning using a frog green scented grub.

fish as far as one hundred feet or more to the side, while pulling lures one hundred feet, or further, behind the boat. This is a proven fish-catching tactic and these smaller, in-line sideplaners are increasing in popularity with the ultralight angler.

To catch bigger, smarter, more wary fish...disassociate terminal tackle from boat and engine noise. FOOL 'EM!

7. SIDEPLANERS/HORIZONTAL HUNTING

"Use sideplaners to intercept fish that are spooked to the sides."

This very effective method of trolling allows anglers to present terminal tackle to fish that are usually not seen on the fish locator. The "stealth" feature of a sideplaner enables an angler to fish in prime waters and intercept many of the fish spooked as the boat passed by. A sideplaner assists the troller to cover more surface acres by placing line and terminal tackle up to 100 feet, or more, to the side of the boat. Another important bonus is the opportunity for the angler to send sideplaner and lure in tight to shore, in "big fish country", keeping the boat at a safe distance from shore without spooking fish. Sideplaners have made trolling with multiple lines much easier and provide anglers with the opportunity to catch more and bigger fish.

Cannon's dual mast system in action.

Several manufacturers offer small "in-line"—stays on your fishing line—sideplaners that are quite inexpensive. Small, lightweight and simple to use, these products have introduced the ultralight concept to sideplaning. Miniplaners, ranging from just five to eight inches in length, enable an angler to easily run lines to each side of the boat to get to places where fish are holding and feeding. The simplicity and ease of use of SEP's Pro SidePlaner, plus its high-visibility fluorescent red color, has made it popular with anglers!

Imagine an early morning on a favorite lake…sitting comfortably in the

Sep's Side Planer—small and light weight, gets out to the sides, just like the larger models.

boat, quietly trolling 100 feet from shore in forty feet of water. The lure is slowly being trolled 90 feet to the side of the boat, five feet below the surface and only TEN feet from shore, in prime water! Simple and effective, sideplaners put offerings where the fish are, without spooking them!

More elaborate sideplaners are available and Cannon has a six-foot Big Boom Mast and dual collapsible Plane-R-Boards which allow lines to be let up to 150 feet to both sides of the boat. It is also possible to run FOUR or more lines on each Plane-R-Board line. Let's see…eight lines on sideplaners…two out the back of the boat…totaling ten lines. That's certainly covering the water and one way to reach more fish!

Try experimenting with a sideplaner and an extra line or two. It takes coordination and a little getting used to, but it is definitely worth it. The sideplaner gets reeled in with the fish, but the extra weight is worth it…the fish would not have been caught unless the lure was out there, attached to the sideplaner, away from the side of the boat.

Just a reminder: keep an eye on other trollers around you, or you'll catch more than you bargained for!

SIDEPLANING

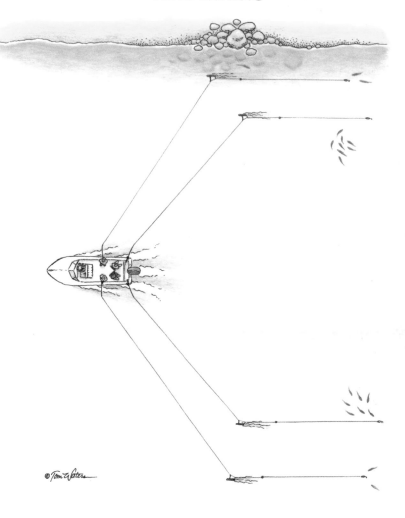

When fish are holding near the surface, match
sidefinder technology with sideplaners
for deadly effective results.

8. VERTICAL HUNTING

"Sometimes you have to work to catch fish."

The electronic technology available today can certainly help unlock the combination to success. However, it is not always easy!

We taught ourselves a lesson years ago while fishing in what appeared to be perfect top-water conditions. We were trolling at a good speed, approximately one mph, and had set out lines 100 feet back. Ideal surface temperatures of 55-58 degrees indicated there should be good numbers of fish near the surface but they were small, few and far between. With an array of flashers, dodgers and small minnow-imitating lures, running from the surface down to fifteen feet, we trolled for several hours, but only a couple of small rainbow trout showed for the effort.

We continued to troll on top...until the locator indicated scattered fish, suspended in very deep 80 to 120 feet of water. It was time to pay closer attention to what the fish locator was signaling and time to "work" the electric downriggers...it was "technology time". To catch fish... would require working for them.

Fishing tackle distributor, Bob Smalley, obviously at the right depth to connect with these two rainbows.

As each and every fish was marked on the fish locator, the downriggers were adjusted. Those fish were chased...wherever they were... the downriggers were raised and lowered to intercept fish from the surface down to 120 feet. By trolling offerings 100 feet behind the boat, we disassociated terminal tackle from the boat, engine and exhaust noises. Even more importantly, it allowed critical time to make necessary depth changes before the lures passed slightly above fish. The short time it took to adjust downrigger depths allowed the lures to pass very close to the holding fish.

These deeper fish were immediately found to be more active. They were bigger too, and obviously not recent planter trout. They could be clearly seen on the fish locator, streaking up from the depths to take a look at the offerings. These fish were holding and actively feeding, and chased trolled baits in the deeper water, striking with voracity. The success rate increased three-fold! In the next three hours, fifteen fish…rainbows and brown trout

Sep lowering downrigger into the zone.

to four pounds, and landlocked king salmon to five pounds, were caught and released.

We refer to this constant adjusting technique as "vertical hunting". Since this first experience, the tactic has proven to work very successfully time after time. It is a practical approach and it works. By simply letting today's technology assist, fish are caught on days that other anglers may call "slow".

We have used a similar technique to catch kokanee salmon late in the season when they were tightly schooled and easy to see on the locator. We watched the locator closely as kokanee, in the eighteen to twenty inch range, followed offerings, without striking. The lures were set ten feet behind the downrigger ball, enabling us to turn tight and troll back through the schools. However, the kokanee would not bite. We decided to try to "tease" the kokanee to strike. The downriggers were raised and lowered rapidly, three to five feet each time, thereby changing the speed, depth, direction and action of the lures. This quickly provoked strikes from the irritated, or tempted, kokanee! "Teasing" has turned many a slow fishing day into fast action and productive angling.

"Vertical Hunting" and "Teasing"…just food for thought!

9. TIME AND DAYS

"Larger, more wary fish get big by being smart."

Every day, first light and dusk are generally peak angling times. Dedicated anglers know that the "right" time always includes being on the water in the very early morning hours. Minnows, baitfish and game fish move to feeding areas and slowly, but methodically, create a food chain throughout the lake. As the first rays of light illuminate the sky, fish species become more active, searching out forage as well as eluding predators that may consider them a meal too. Dusk offers anglers another prime opportunity to intercept feeding fish and many times the evening bite far surpasses the morning bite.

However, do not be lulled into a morning/evening program. Fish will go on and off the bite several times each day and anglers can often miss prime time angling by restricting their activities to morning and evening fishing only.

In lakes where legal, fishing at night can often be the most productive time for big fish. German brown trout and rainbows drop their guard in the safety of darkness. Being primarily nocturnal feeders, bigger, more wary trout get big by being smart.

For years, we have kept a diary of our fishing excursions and this has proven invaluable in planning upcoming trips. Recurring entries clearly advise...NEVER, EVER fish on a full moon...obviously written after countless hours of angling frustration on the water. We have found that the best fishing occurs on a new or no-moon phase, or when the moon is so low on the horizon that it shines only a short period of time before disappearing. Out of necessity, however, we have not always been able to take our own advice.

What is it about a full moon that causes fishing to slow? There are many theories on the subject, including tides, gravitational pull of the earth and moon, specific feeding peri-

Albert Castano with rainbow trout, caught mid-day.

ods, and our favorite...the "bright full-moon, lit skies" theory. Basically, it goes like this. Fish see up. On bright moonlit nights, from below, trout can easily spot silhouettes of minnows or baitfish against the light surface. These easy pickings mean stuffed fish by dawn. By sunrise, the angler is fishing for trout that have been eating all night long. Make sense? It only figures that the best fishing would be on a new or no-moon...right? Maybe!

Generally, the period three days before a new moon and up to seven days afterward seems to produce the best action. We try to plan our trips accordingly with the use of a moon-phase calendar. To the contrary however, we have had phenomenal fishing success during bright moon periods. How do you figure? Over-all, there is certainly a correlation between a new moon and good fishing, but these periods too, are affected by fluctuating barometric pressure and approaching storms or low pressure conditions. Certainly, variables such as these, plus cloudy skies and wind, have to be dealt with. Alone, or in combination, each will have an impact on angling success.

Oncoming storms and low pressure may bring wind, rain and rough conditions. Those prepared to adapt tactics, gear and clothing can intercept the fish of a lifetime.

The single most important factor deciding the fate of a day of fishing, is the CHANGE IN BAROMETRIC PRESSURE. Rapidly changing barometric pressure often puts fish off the bite. Dropping barometric pressure signals a weather change or the arrival of a storm front. Rising pressure indicates the onset of high pressure or clearing weather. Quite often during these fluctuations, fish seem to get...lockjaw! When the barometric pressure bounces like a seismograph during an earthquake, select the days to go fishing very carefully. The day may look "fishable", but your quarry may ignore offerings for any number of reasons. Just let that pressure settle down and stabilize for a couple of days in a row, and angling becomes far more productive.

Anglers who can be flexible to plan trips conveniently around storms and changing barometric pressure will have better results. Unfortunately, storm fronts do not know or care about days off from work and anglers may be forced to fish on days when the pressure is dropping significantly. The day may look perfect initially, but as the front approaches from hundreds of miles away, the change in pressure is certainly detected by fish. They tend to shut down, possibly in anticipation of an impending storm.

It is frustrating, getting "skunked" and it happens to everyone. It is expensive, and even more importantly, uses up limited and valuable leisure time. Anglers want their chosen trips to be successful. The best way to do this is to let the high and low pressures stabilize, preferably letting a high settle in for a couple of days before heading out. If you can be flexible on dates, it pays off! Wait for the right day, when at least a couple of things are favorable, then give it your best shot. Under questionable conditions, troll deeper, and search for moving, actively feeding fish. When the pressure is dropping, fish will drop, too.

In spite of frosty downriggers and frozen line, morning's first light can be the most productive.

Let's take the subject one step further, a useful tool to help pinpoint the exact time of day to expect to find the best fishing, and hunting, periods, is a small, thirty-two page paperback book. John Alden Knight's "*Solunar Tables*" forecasts the daily feeding times of fish and game, for every day of the year. Each day is broken down into two or three peak opportunity periods that often last several hours. By Region, it defines the window of maximum opportunity for anglers and hunters.

Similar to tide tables, it spells out periods when the moon alignment is directly overhead, or underfoot. This "*Moon-Up/Moon-Down*", theory has been proven by outdoorsmen, both in the field and on the water, for over sixty years. There are periods, where for no particular reason, action breaks loose. We have all had those great days…is it luck, or just being persistent? Chances are, if you were to check out Knight's "*Tables*", you would find a direct correlation between the action and the predicted peak periods. It may not always be totally right-on, but its accuracy has surprised even seasoned anglers.

We have been skeptical about the tables…but have used and verified them enough now to have considerable confidence in their accuracy. They really do seem to work and if you're like us, you need all the help you can get! The tables are probably available at your favorite tackle shop. A bigger book, called "*Moon-Up/Moon-Down*" by Knight, the originator of the Solunar Theory, details the background and development of the tables. It just comes down to the fact that for one of a hundred reasons, you either catch fish, or you don't. And remember, just being there is half the fun. We've had lots of great "fishing trips" when we've been skunked!

Late evening near dusk is good too, as these two anglers prove.

10. TURNOVER TIME

Timing is everything.

Each year, normally during the early fall period, freshwater trout anglers anxiously and often impatiently await the arrival of the "turnover". It is no wonder! With turnover comes some of the best and possibly most exciting fishing opportunities of the year. Turnover, however, is a short-lived process and knowledgeable anglers know they must be ready to act.

Simply put...turnover is the process of "hypolimniation". It is that brief period of time brought on by the arrival of fall, when lake waters intermix and create the same temperature from top to bottom.

A combination of temperature change, wind and weather creates the upwelling inversion of water. This annual process consistently brings game fish and bait to the surface at the same time. As the water and weather temperatures continue to cool, the nutrient and oxygen rich waters of the "thermocline" rise to the surface. This brings trout and salmon to the surface, too, where plankton, minnows and other naturally occurring meals are readily available. Generally, turnover conditions produce wide-open bites when trout concentrate in the top twenty feet of water and larger holdover fish can be caught. As temperatures continue to drop, fishing will steadily improve, and then peak. The lake will restratify and trout and salmon, searching out their ideal temperature range, will subsequently be found at varying depths.

Starting first at higher elevation lakes, turnover will normally last from a few days to a few weeks before the arrival of winter. The water of the lake will slowly begin to restratify

Cold weather, cold water and wind, bring trophy-sized trout to the surface. Sep with a 4-pound trout, caught top-lining.

into the normal layers of the "epilimnium" (surface waters), "thermocline" (ideal temperature range), and "hypolimnium" (oxygen and nutrient-poor, deeper waters). Ideal temperatures, plus oxygenated and nutrient-rich waters provide "easy pickings", and puts turnover fish and anglers alike, in an aggressive frenzy. Fishing success will vary, eventually slowing down considerably as restratification takes place.

Check on favorite lakes to find out approximately when turnover will occur and plan trips accordingly.

Gary Davis with two 4 1/2-pound rainbows caught in early fall, during turnover.

Marina operators and guides are well aware of conditions and will gladly share information. We always anxiously await the coming of turnover and the fall fishing season as it marks the beginning of great angling opportunities for trophy-sized fish. They are actively on the prowl, feeding frequently in an effort to build body fat to hold them through the cold winter months. This is the time that a properly presented bait or lure is likely to catch that one fish of a lifetime!

Fred Andriano with 6-pound "turnover" trout.

11. ALTERNATIVES

Trolling isn't always the answer!

As turnover occurs, trollers temporarily set aside the use of downriggers and electronics and begin "top-lining" for trout. This long-line presentation of lures or trolled baits pulled shallow, about 100 feet behind the boat, is one of the best ways to enjoy the fight of a battling rainbow trout. If trolling lures, it is important they are about the same size as the minnows in the lake, generally about one inch long. White or pearl colored lures are good producers because of their resemblance to minnows, the primary food source of trout. The addition of attractors such as flashers or dodgers will certainly enhance the presentation. Troll slowly, about one mph, off the main body of the lake, around points and drop-offs. Look for areas where there is less traffic and activity and therefore better fishing.

MATCH YOUR TACKLE TO THE TASK! Use a casting or spinning rod and reel combination loaded with six to eight pound test line. A threaded nightcrawler or a lip-hooked minnow, (where legal), trolled slowly behind small flashers will produce fish. Live bait presentation is tricky…when you feel the bite, drop the rod tip back toward the fish and control the urge to set the hook. Let the fish hold on to the bait and the next time you feel movement, set the hook.

There are a couple of other common techniques that shore fishermen or anglers stillfishing from a boat can consider. Try utilizing a sliding or slip bobber and ultralight tackle. A six to seven foot light-action spinning rod, equipped with a spinning reel with four to eight pound test line is perfect. When fish are suspended above the lake bottom or there are numerous snags and weed growth, bobber-stop devices enable the angler to set the exact depth of the offering.

The sliding sinker method places the offering on or near the bottom of the lake. It presents bait in such a manner that fish do not detect, until it is too late, that it is attached to a rod and reel, and an angler. Cast out the desired distance that you think will intercept fish. With a spinning reel, leave the bail open so the line can move freely through the sliding sinker, allowing the fish to "hit and run", with the bait. After the bait has been taken and the fish begins to move off, slowly close the bail and wait for the line to tighten. Just as the rod begins to bend with the pull of the fish…set the hook. Just give a single, short, firm set. It is not necessary to "rip the lips" off the fish to set the hook!

A threaded nightcrawler on a size 4 or 6 hook, or a dorsal-hooked minnow, where legal, simply cast out to drift is a deadly offering. While waiting

A threaded night crawler can be deadly.

for a hit, keep the bail open on the reel…a trout can feel minimal resistance as it takes the bait and hook. Wait to feel the pull of the fish before setting the hook. Handle the rod carefully and calmly. This technique allows the fish to move off with the bait without knowing the offering is attached to rod and reel. A premature set of the hook will only result in a missed fish. Control the excitement and wait until the rod bends…then set the hook…if you can wait that long!

In lakes where weeds grow heavily from the bottom, successful anglers use methods that float offerings above the weed beds. Nightcrawlers can be inflated with a worm-blower, available in most tackle shops. Another method is to first thread a nightcrawler on the hook, and then attach a mini-marshmallow on the barb. This technique has definitely been refined with the introduction of floating baits as the added buoyancy is all it takes to raise the offering several feet off the bottom.

No matter how we personally feel, trolling is not always the answer to connecting with fish. Anglers just might want to be prepared to still-fish or cast from boat or shore if absolutely necessary! With any of these "soft-bait" techniques, remember…do not set the hook too soon, or too hard or you will soon be re-rigging your bait instead of fighting a fish!

12. TROLLING SPEED

Slow trolling catches more fish.

Best results are generally obtained trolling between one-half and 1-1/2 mph. Proper speed is very important for maximum lure action to entice fish to strike. Too slow...and lure action may be dead. Too fast...and the fish may not want to expend the energy to pursue it. Vary trolling speed, particularly when action is slow. Also, it's a good idea to give an occasional spurt of power to the engine. There are times that a cautious fish can be enticed to strike by the speeded up action of the lure.

Fish in the thermocline will be the most active, so an angler can afford to troll a little faster. If fishing above or below the thermocline, whether the temperature is warmer or cooler, troll slower. Fish in these areas are saving energy and will not waste it in a high-speed chase. Slow trolled minnow-imitating lures can be deadly effective on foraging trout because they match the size and shape of natural food sources in the lake. On the other hand, when fishing is slow, search for that "impulse strike", by fast trolling larger lures at two to four mph, top-water or on downriggers, with or without attractors.

Don't be afraid to troll multiple lines, just watch your turns. Seven lines out—four just below the surface on downriggers, two on sideplaners and one on top down the middle.

Troll in exaggerated "S" turns. Every experienced troller has seen it happen any number of times...make a turn and hook up a fish! Consider this...you are fishing with two rods and you make a turn. The lure on the inside rod slows down and DROPS deeper, while the lure on the outside rod speeds up and RISES to a shallower depth. The inside rod hooks a fish!

"S" TROLLING PATTERN

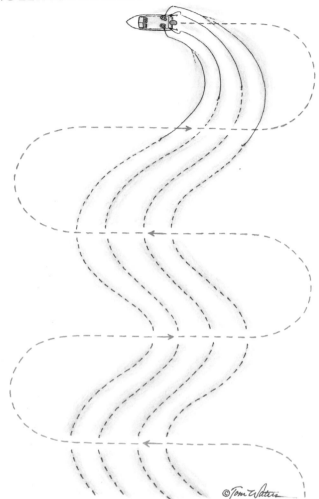

©Tom Waters

The "S" turns allow the angler to cover not only more water, but the ability to place lures or bait at varying depths at once. It is a great tactic to catch fish because it automatically varies depth, speed and lure action.

Too many lines? In recent years, many States have initiated a "second rod" stamp to be added to a regular fishing license. When this happened in California... no problem, we thought. Instead of our usual two lines, we could now run four on the downriggers, all set at varying depths. This works fine when there are only two of us on board, but what happens when there are three or four anglers wanting to fish...SIX lines, or more? Maybe!

TROLLING SPEED

A bow-mounted electric trolling motor offers better control at slow speeds.

It is possible to easily troll five, six or more lines on the surface behind the boat, but making turns can be a lesson in weaving and braiding monofilament line. Therefore, it is important to stagger or vary the lengths of the lines so they do not overlap and tangle on turns. Put longer lines on the outside and shorter ones down the middle to reduce tangles and to allow a tighter turning radius. We have successfully trolled six or seven rods in the past without too much trouble, but you can bet we did not make any exaggerated "S" turns!

Cold enough? Marilyn slowed down to catch this lethargic 5-pound rainbow.

Traditionally, some of the largest trout of the year are caught during the cooler winter months. For cold weather success, anglers need to adjust trolling techniques, especially speed. First of all, it is COLD! When water temperatures drop considerably, trout become increasingly lethargic. The impact of this cooling should not be taken lightly. As water temperatures drop below the ideal 52- to 58-degree range, trout and salmon will seek out shallower sun-warmed waters. Their metabolism, digestion and feeding patterns slow in an attempt to conserve energy. They are less likely to move any great distance and will not expend the energy needed to chase down their prey. Instead, they will wait in ambush for food that drifts or floats by within their attack range. It is the angler's job to attempt to provoke that impulse strike by finding the correct combination of vibration, color and most importantly, speed.

13. LINE AND LEADER

Light line and leader are a must.

Keep it LIGHT, to enjoy the fight of the fish. Basically, four to eight pound test line on a six- to seven-foot medium action rod will handle fish from one to ten pounds with ease.

Use high-quality, abrasion-resistant, small-diameter monofilament lines. When trolling, or stillfishing, in freshwater lakes, correct line size depends on four main factors:

- Size and variety of game fish being targeted
- Casting or spinning rod and reel being used
- Pound test line recommended for the rod
- Most important…level of skill and experience of the angler

Most freshwater lakes produce planted trout averaging one to two pounds in size. However, there is always the possibility of a trophy-sized specimen coming by and hammering the offering. Be prepared for such situations.

Many of the waters we troll produce trout from two to six pounds. Even so, we stick to lighter monofilaments. When using spinning equipment, we prefer six-pound test on our reels and four-pound leader of equal quality material. For level-wind or casting rods and reels, we upgrade to eight-pound test, with leaders of six-pound test. This allows us to troll faster with heavier trolling rigs or with larger lures that have greater resistance.

One of the disadvantages of using monofilament line is the "stretch factor", most lines rated at ten percent. With 150 feet of line out behind the boat…that translates into fifteen feet of stretch in the line…sometimes making it difficult to feel the initial strike.

The new era in lines such as Spiderwire, Fireline and Gorilla Braid are all minimal stretch lines. Whereas monofilament can stretch up to ten percent before breaking, these new lines have a maximum stretch of just two percent. With ultra-low stretch and virtually no memory (coiling), these lines deliver maximum sensitivity and firmer, faster hook-setting force. An angler can readily feel every head jerk and movement generated by a fish because of the minimum stretch feature of these lines.

A high-quality rod, offering good flexibility, matched with a quality reel equipped with a smooth-acting drag system can absorb a great deal of the shock when fighting even the largest of fish. It is possible to fight a fish that is considerably heavier than the line strength, if the drag on the reel is

SEP'S 4/O PRO DODGER AND KOKANEE KANDY LURE

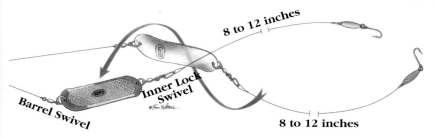

8 to 12 inches

Inner Lock Swivel

Barrel Swivel

8 to 12 inches

adjusted properly. This means…let the ROD and DRAG SYSTEM work for you. Set the drag properly and check periodically to be sure it has not changed. Keep in mind, there should be little, if any, sound of the drag working as you reel. The pump and reel technique, "pump up gently, reel down slowly", done correctly, creates very little sound and means you are doing it right!

Another important consideration in selecting line strength is the size of the teeth of the fish you are after and the damage they could do to the leader. For instance, if hunting big trophy rainbow or brown trout, adjust upwards accordingly, such as to ten-pound test or more.

Anglers should not overlook the importance of low visibility when selecting fishing lines. Remember, fish look up and see objects, including fishing line, against a light surface. Fishing line colors of green and gray are the least visible to fish. Fluorescent clear blues are often highly visible and appear almost neon from below.

Leader Length

The appropriate leader length is unquestionably important. When trolling a bare lure, use at least a 36-inch leader and a swivel to help prevent line twist. However, all that changes when adding attractor flashers or dodgers to enhance the action and vibration of the lure.

Behind flashers, use an 18- to 24-inch leader, particularly when using a rubber snubber as a leader shock absorber. Some anglers prefer longer leaders, sometimes as much as 24-48 inches, when pulling flashers. Our feeling is that fish are attracted first to the churning blades, rather than the trailing lure. After all, the blades do create the fish-attracting vibrations and the lure should be enticingly close behind.

When using a small 4/0 dodger to enhance the action and vibration of the lure, use just eight to twelve inches of leader. The formula for leader length in this case, is two to three times the length of the dodger. 4/0 dodgers are four inches long…the correct leader length would be eight to twelve inches. If the leader is too short, the lure will move so much that a fish may have a hard time catching it. If the leader length is too long, very little of the enhancing action of the dodger will be transmitted to the lure.

Preventing Line Twist

The initial opportunity to have line twist occurs when first spooling up. Line can twist as it comes off the spool and can become a problem even before getting to the water. Try turning the spool and feeding from the front, and the back, to determine which direction causes less twist as line goes on to the spool of the reel.

Another trick to reduce line problems is, once the reel is spooled up, take it outside, and tie the loose end of the line to a fixed object. Walk back, keeping tension on the line. After letting out about fifty yards, pull on the line a bit to stretch it. This makes the line much easier to work with when fishing.

When using "casting" rods and reels, there is relatively little opportunity for line twist, one of the main reasons they are so popular with beginning and experienced anglers. "Spinning" reels are the real culprits when it comes to twisting, but their twists are generally operator caused errors.

Reeling Against the Drag

This is undoubtedly the most common way to get unwanted line twist. When retrieving offerings or fighting a fish, it is important to not reel "against the drag". If a fish is taking out line and you are reeling in at the same time, line twist is definitely being created. Each rotation reeled against the drag of a 5:1 ratio reel, will put five twists in the line.

Let the fish run when it is stripping line...do not reel against the drag. Using a "pump and reel" retrieval will help reduce the major cause of line twist. Pull back slowly with the rod, bringing in as much line as comfortably possible. Then, without lessening the pressure, reel in and take up line, while moving forward with the rod. PUMP AND REEL! If you can hear the sound of the drag as you reel, stop reeling. Use the rod as leverage and as you "pump and reel" correctly, there will be very little drag noise and very little line twist.

Trolling too fast is another easy way to create problems. If trolling speed is such that the lure, bait or attractors rotate faster than the swivels will allow...this too will cause line twist.

Choose line carefully...and use quality, no matter how few times a year you fish. Line connects you to your fish and wouldn't you be angry losing a big one because line or leader broke? Knots are important too, and if you aren't totally positive about the knots you have tied, re-do them! There are many uncontrollable variables out there and you certainly do not need to question the quality of line or knots while trolling.

Replace line and leader regularly and often. Sometimes replace line every other day, depending upon how much time is spent on the water! Anglers should check for nicks and abrasions when letting out line. Get in the habit of letting the line slide through your fingers and feel for irregularities.

Here's a suggestion...after trolling most of the day, an angler might notice that the line has become quite twisted. It is possible to undo many of the twists rather

Col. Lou Newfield slow-trolled a 4/0 dodger in deep water for these kokanee salmon.

easily. Slowly head across the water and take all the hardware, including swivels, off the line. Let out line for 100 feet or so and drag it along for several minutes. Bring it slowly back onto the reel. The majority of the twists will be gone. This might save re-spooling and will certainly save valuable fishing time in the long run.

Think about what is happening to lures or bait while trolling along. Line strength, density, color and variety have been created for some reason. Try to utilize the correct application for your specific purpose. The results will surely pay off, with more time in the water. After all, it is the angler who has line in the water longer than another who catches more fish!

14. VIBRATIONS AND ATTRACTORS

Fish are attracted first by vibrations.

Every species of fish has an extended row of nerves that runs the length of its body. These nerve endings are referred to as the "lateral line sensors". To a fish, this is their sense of touch in the water. They can detect vibrations fifty feet or more away, depending upon weather and water conditions. In calm, undisturbed water, fish can "feel" further…and the troller has "attract-ability" from greater distances. In churned up water, fish often go into a feeding frenzy when minnows and baitfish become disoriented. This is why there is often an improved bite just as the wind begins to whip up the lake.

Fish are attracted first by the vibrations created from trolled offerings. In many cases, trolling is tremendously enhanced by the use of attractor blades, or flashers…and "flashers" is actually a misnomer! It is the "vibrations" created by the blades, not the "flashes", which initially attract fish. As fish are attracted and move nearer, they rely on their sense of sight, and move in closer when they spot the flashes. Their sense of smell then takes over as they key on bait or scented lures. Their eyesight is so poor that they do not detect colors until they are nearly upon the offerings.

SEP'S ultralight trolling flashers were designed for optimum fishing enjoyment! These small and lightweight trolling blades move through the water with little resistance and do not spook fish with excessive flashes and vibrations. They were designed to produce smaller vibrations when trolled slowly, similar to those of minnows and baitfish. Less offensive vibrations and flashes attract fish, enticing them to strike lures or bait. Also, the conventional, large flashers pull heavily on the rod, reel and line, and at times an angler can have a fish on and not even know it! A long time ago, we realized it is far more fun to play a fish with less drag on the line. "FEEL THE FIGHT…IT'S ULTRALIGHT" became SEP'S company motto!

New additions to the tackle market include Mini Micro flashers by SEP'S.

Marilyn used a small 4/0 dodger to catch this spring-time rainbow.

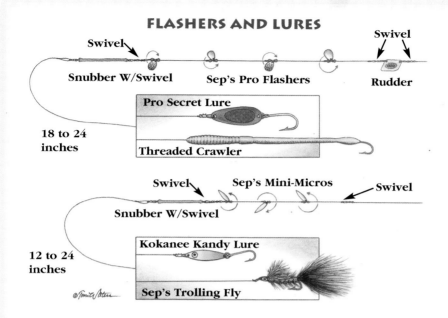

FLASHERS AND LURES

Swivel • Snubber W/Swivel • Sep's Pro Flashers • Swivel • Rudder • 18 to 24 inches • Pro Secret Lure • Threaded Crawler • Swivel • Sep's Mini-Micros • Swivel • Snubber W/Swivel • 12 to 24 inches • Kokanee Kandy Lure • Sep's Trolling Fly

These truly miniature and ultralight trolling flashers were designed to provide maximum vibrations from the lightest, most compact blades available. They have very little drag. At times, when just the slightest vibration or attraction is called for, when fish are spooked and hit very lightly, these smallest of flashers can be very effective. Plus, they're not just for trollers…this flasher system is also "castable" and can be utilized from shore.

Which shape of blades produces the most vibrations as they are trolled through the water? The strongest vibrations, which can be felt farthest away by a fish's lateral line sensors, are created by the round "Colorado" shaped blades. "Tear-drop", or "Indiana" blades produce the next strongest vibrations. The weakest of the vibrations are created by the narrow "Willow-leaf" shaped blades. Which is the best to use? The one that is catching fish!

Flashers create vibrations but do little to enhance lure action. The dodger, an alternative attractor, creates vibration and more action, in addition to enhancing the movement of the lure. When trolled at slow speed, the dodger transmits a swimming, surging action to the lure or bait that many fish find irresistible. The side-to-side erratic motion produces action that causes strikes. Small 4/0 dodgers and the small tear-drop shaped, "Side-Kick" dodgers are lightweight and very effective. Both types of products increase the action and/or vibrations of terminal offerings and definitely attract fish.

It is best to troll slowly and to diversify offerings, tactics and techniques. As your fishing day begins, vary equipment on the rods, utilizing either

Flashers attached to the downrigger ball can be very effective.

Sep used large painted flashers to fool this kohanee salmon—vibration and color are key.

flashers or dodgers. After a fish or two is caught, re-rig to the most successful technique. When that method quits working, switch again.

Clarity of water assists the angler in determining which color of flashers or dodgers to use. A good general rule-of-thumb is to use silver flashers when water is relatively clear. In low light, deep or off-color water, use gold. However, these are just suggestions and results can be obtained either way, perhaps just not as routinely. Certain flashers have colored

SIDE-KICK DODGER AND GRUB

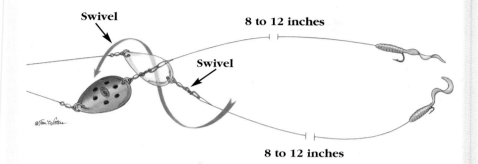

prism tape attached to the blades and this does enhance the flash. Bright, painted blades also have a spot in the troller's tackle box, and are very effective when trolled in very clear water on bright days.

Dodgers come in assorted finishes—silver for clear water, gold or copper for dark, or off-color water. Painted finishes and colored prism tape have major impact when correctly applied to the depths trolled. Reds, oranges and silvers are best used near the surface, where sufficient lighting is present. The colors of gold, blue and green can be seen further underwater and in low light conditions. Chartreuse and pearl are versatile. Glow-in-the-dark dodgers are very effective when trolled at deeper depths.

What about attaching flashers to the downrigger ball, then trolling a bare lure or bait above? This is a relatively common technique, particularly with kokanee trollers, who find it very successful. It allows anglers to fish just a few feet behind the downrigger ball, and is not generally recommended for trout trolling. The flashers, usually made with larger blades, are attached to the downrigger weight, eliminating the "in-line" aspect. This reduces the drag even more. Simply let out five to ten feet of line and connect to the release, about three feet above the weight and flashers. The vibrations of the flashers attract and excite fish, which then hopefully, hit the lure in the process.

Indiana Blade

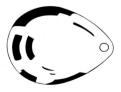

Colorado Blade

Willowleaf Blade

15. LURES...COLORS

Depth helps to determine which color to use.

Do fish see color? Do they select food sources of one color over other colors? Studies have been done over the years and fish apparently have the cells and pigments needed to be able to see color, but they, like us, do not see colors well in low light conditions. It is known they can distinguish different shades of color and the most involved research we have read states that blue and green are strong favorites.

Some basic guidelines regarding color choices:
- On bright sun-shiny days with clear water conditions, use silver lures
- On dark or overcast days, gold is recommended
- Brightly painted lures are by far the most visible
- Colors of red, orange and pink, (sunrise and sunset colors), are best used near the surface in the top thirty feet or so, depending on water clarity and available light
- White and shades of green and blue are effective in deeper, darker water where there is less light penetration
- Chartreuse and pearl are consistent producers, no matter at what depth.

It is action and vibration that initially attract fish. When slow trolling at speeds of one half to one mph, use lures that imitate the minnows and bait-

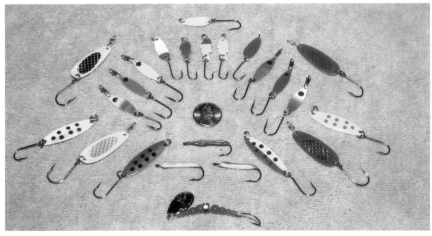

Trout and kokanee lures from various manufacturers offer plenty of choices of colors, shapes, sizes and actions.

fish in the lake. Fish are limited in what they eat by the size of their mouths. Larger trout with larger mouths can take much larger food sizes than small trout can. Think about this when selecting which lure to use. Check the action of the lure by observing it on the line, in the water alongside the boat before letting it out all the way. Ensure the action is smooth and correct. Some lures require "tuning "or bending and even a swivel can sometimes alter the performance or action of the lure.

Check the movement of threaded nightcrawlers, minnows, lures or trolled flies and grubs to ensure they run true and "slither" through the water without twisting the line. Slight adjustments in hook direction can generally correct irregular movements. A worm threader or a threading needle can simplify rigging.

Minnow-imitating, lightweight, flutter-type lures such as the Pro Secret, Kokanee Kandy, Bantam Cyclops, Needlefish, Dick Nite, and more, offer maximum action and vibration when trolled at slow speeds. Their appearance, presentation and action

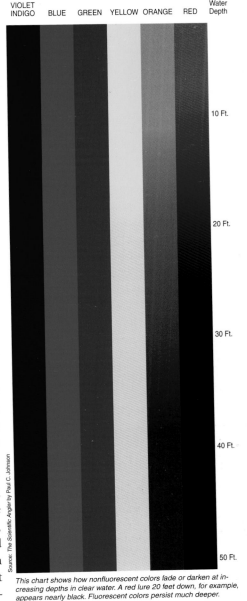

Source: *The Scientific Angler by Paul C. Johnson*

SEP HENDRICKSON

This chart shows how nonfluorescent colors fade or darken at increasing depths in clear water. A red lure 20 feet down, for example, appears nearly black. Fluorescent colors persist much deeper.

make them very effective. Lures in various colors with prism tape offer a scale-like appearance that matches natural food sources. Lures available in chrome, gold plate, copper or brightly painted finishes offer high visibility under water.

When fishing for kokanee, always tip the barb of the hook with white corn—not yellow, WHITE! No one really knows why it works, but this "magic" can make or break a kokanee fishing day. Some anglers say it works because it is a maggot imitation, while others think it creates a scent path, or it looks or smells like plankton, primary food source of the kokanee. Anglers do catch kokanee by placing a small piece of night-crawler on the hook, but undoubtedly, the angler using the white corn will outfish them all!

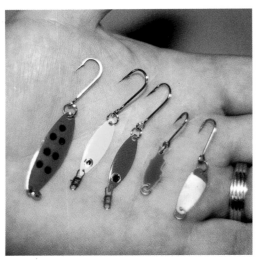

Left to right: Needlefish, Kokanee Kandy, Triple Teaser and Dick Nite spoons all come in a wide variety of fish-attracting colors.

Scents can effectively be mixed into the corn, and "mad scientist" fishermen often create concoctions they swear no fish can refuse! For example, some anglers mix corn and anise, minnow or crawfish together to create their own fish attracting cocktail. Mr. Twister manufactures Exude corn, which like its name suggests, exudes scent upon contact with the water. It comes in several colors and looks just like corn, plus it's durable and stays on the hook.

Finding the correct combination of action, vibration and colors of lures is not easy, do not be reluctant to change lures.

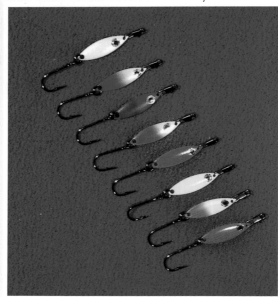

Kokanee salmon prefer small brightly-colored lures, such as Sep's Kokanee Kandy.

16. COMMON SENSE ON SCENTS

There is no doubt that scents work!

A wide variety of manufactured scents or attractants, each with a distinctive odor and individual success rate, are available to sport fishermen. It is confirmed that trout and salmon can sense small amounts of chemicals in large bodies of water.

Fish attractants do three things:
- Most important, they mask human scent. Oils and smells produced naturally by human bodies can repel fish and keep them from striking. Trout and salmon species have a keen sense of smell and may turn away from lures that carry normal human odors, or unnatural scents created by tobacco, gasoline, cologne, perfume, strong soap, etc.
- Attractants create "scent paths" that entice fish to follow a lure or bait. A trolling angler can create an attractant trail that prowling fish may intercept and follow, thinking they are closing in on an easy meal.
- Because of the natural smell and taste of the scented lure or bait, a fish may hit and hold on to it longer, providing additional seconds for the angler to "stick" the fish and set the hook.

There is no doubt that scents work. On most days, using scents can improve angling action dramatically. At times, we have trolled awhile, without catching a fish and then realized we had not applied scent. After

Scents make sense.

applying attractant, a fish has been caught almost immediately! Is this just dumb luck or the effect of the scent just used? We prefer to think it is the attractant!

Always go fishing with a wide variety of "smells". They come in many "flavors", including crayfish, anchovy, shrimp, sardine, herring, nightcrawler, anise, corn, garlic, and more. Attractants come in many forms and can be applied by spraying on, pouring on, wiping on, rubbing on, etc.

We've had consistent success using Smelly Jelly, a thick odiferous jell, produced by Catcher

Dawn Suliak caught this mid-summer rainbow trout using scent on her lure.

Company. It is available in a wide variety of natural bait odors, is biodegradable and works on all baits and lures. Pro Cure manufactures other widely used products that are the "real" thing...ground up! Names like Predator, Fish Oil and Bait Butter are well-known favorites among trollers. An application of these scent products will last for several hours. As a matter of fact, they last so well that it is recommended wiping lures clean before placing them back into the tackle box.

There are also products that remove scents instead of creating them. Most odor eliminators are biodegradable and easy to use on hands and skin. They can be used on fishing and hunting equipment, cutting boards, countertops etc. We have the scents, smells and flavors to entice fish, plus methods of removing scents from our hands, but do we have the "sense" to use them?

Anglers Tom and Kim Coster increased their odds of hook-ups by using scents.

17. TROLLING FLIES

Draggin' flies works!

When fall "turnover" is complete and surface waters have cooled considerably, fish of all species begin to feed heavily in preparation for the harsh winter months ahead. Instinctively, feeding and building fat reserves, "energy", becomes the top priority of the fish. Trout and salmon will pursue a wide variety of food sources but it is the minnow or baitfish that offers the most energy per meal...and fish know it.

When presented properly, one of the most realistic minnow imitations is the trolling fly. Available in a wide variety of fish-attracting colors and designs, trolling flies that imitate minnows, or leeches, emergers and other natural baits are excellent producers. Used in place of lures, spoons or nightcrawlers, flies are proven producers because they move realistically, imitating natural food sources.

SIDE-KICK DODGER AND FLY

8 to 12 inches

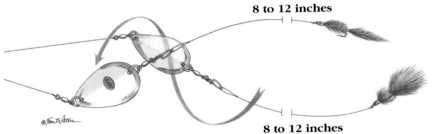

8 to 12 inches

Trolling flies are effective, versatile and fun. They can be trolled top-line by themselves, but the angler must create the fish-attracting action, by methodically and consistently twitching or pumping the rod tip to pass action to the fly. An erratic figure-eight design, drawn with the rod tip also creates a most effective attractor. Repeating and varying this action creates the realistic motion the fish is looking for before it strikes.

Flies can be effectively trolled behind flashers for spectacular results at times. They can also be deadly effective when top-lined behind small 4/0 dodgers. The side-to-side action and vibration of the dodger imparts an enticing swimming, surging action to the fly that attracts fish. The addition of a dodger also adds weight, which takes the offering down slightly deeper. To get even more depth, use downriggers, diving planes or weights, but the fly's reaction is solely dependent upon the flasher or dodger leading the way.

Trolling flies are extremely effective when top-lined with sideplaners. The preferred technique is to let line and trolling fly out approximately 100

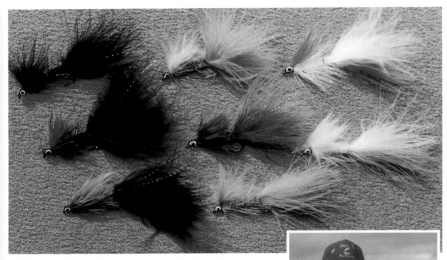

When trolling flies, try to match the colors with natural food sources in the lake.

Paul Hendrickson with a trout caught using a black/olive trolling fly.

feet behind the boat, then to connect the line to the sideplaner. Let the sideplaner run 40-50 feet, or more, to the side of the boat. This gets the offering out to the side, where fish holding near the surface have moved, as the boat passed over them. Sideplaners also enable anglers to get into those close-to-shore, hard to get to spots where fish are cruising in search of a meal.

Far more important though, is the natural action transmitted to the fly as the sideplaner moves and surges through and across the surface of the water. The sideplaner works especially well when trolled in water that has a slight chop or wave action…surging across the surface, the sideplaner naturally imparts the necessary fish attracting action to the fly.

When selecting colors, attempt to imitate the natural food sources found in the lake. Blacks, browns, reds and cinnamon resemble leeches…whites and grays look like minnows, and olives and black/olives bear a startling resemblance to emergers (dragonfly and damselfly nymphs). The vibrant, hot colors of chartreuse, pink, orange and purple are in a class of their own…and often get a reaction when nothing else is working.

The next time you wonder which lure to use, try draggin' flies—they work!

18. TROLLING GRUBS

You may never use a nightcrawler again!

Small two- and three-inch curltail grubs, normally used for panfish or bass fishing, offer anglers a realistic-looking imitation of natural food sources when trolled.

Whether imitating minnows, leeches or aquatic insect life or simple nightcrawlers or worms, properly presented grubs are excellent attractors. Available in a wide variety of colors, grubs move through the water in an enticing, vibrating manner that attracts fish to strike. Much like trolling with flies, running grubs behind flashers, dodgers or sideplaners will increase their effectiveness. Match the color, size and speed of natural food sources available and positive results and hookups will follow.

White grubs imitate minnows. Black is best for freshwater leeches, brown for nightcrawlers or worms and green for minnows and aquatic insects.

PROPER RIGGING OF GRUB

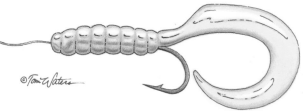

©Tom Waters

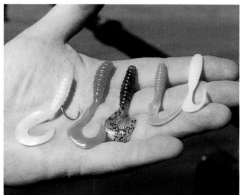

Trolling grubs in a wide variety of colors "match the batch"!

The brighter, more vibrant colors like hot pink, bright orange, chartreuse and purple are also productive because of their visibility in a wide variety of depths and light conditions.

You may never use a nightcrawler again! Black and brown grubs are perfect imitations for nightcrawlers.

Once you have tried using grubs and experienced the results, you will soon experiment with various colors, trolling speeds, the use of downriggers and sideplaners, plus the addition of scents.

Effective? Deadly effective…just give them a chance!

19. HOOK SET

No need to rip the lips.

Warning! Watching too many bass-fishing television shows before going trolling for trout or kokanee is not a good idea!

Many times, an angler will lose a fish because the hook was set with enough force to pull a marlin out of the water! Remember, for the most part, the trout and salmon talked about here are small fish in the 12- to 20-inch range. Even the bigger ones do not need a major hook set...it is not necessary to slam the hook home. All that is required is tightening the line...just cinching it up, plus a light tug, will generally do the trick. Actually, most of the time, especially when trolling, the fish will do it for you!

Using a rubber snubber is recommended when trolling flashers. Anglers will definitely hook and successfully land more trout and salmon using a snubber as it helps to ensure the hook set is not too hard. A snubber gives the line just the right amount of elasticity at the onset of the strike, to keep the line from snapping. It also acts as a shock absorber during the fight. When using flashers and a nightcrawler or grub, or flashers and a lure, attach the snubber just behind the flashers, then clip the leader on to the other end of the snubber.

To vary the action to the lure or bait, attach a small dodger instead of flashers. Kokanee trollers find the use of dodgers to be particularly effective. A dodger will give a surging, swimming action to the offering and a different technique is utilized. A snubber is not recommended for use with a dodger because it deadens the dodger's action as it is transmitted to the lure.

Keep in mind, when a kokanee is hooked up, do not horse it in. Use "finesse". The mouth of a kokanee is very soft and its intense struggle requires the angler to "baby" it to the net. If drag is set too tight or excessive pressure is applied during the fight, the paper-thin mouth will often tear and the fish will escape.

When a kokanee gets close to the boat, it really starts acting "salmon-like". A kokanee will jump, tail-walk and basically go crazy, and the closer it gets to the boat, the harder it fights. This is definitely the time for an angler to be gentle and very

Sep with a "finessed" kokanee.

careful...maintain steady pressure, be patient and above all, enjoy the fight. By the way, more kokanee are lost right at the boat as the angler attempts to net it! Consider using a very long handled net...eight feet of reach often spells the difference between a netted or a lost fish.

20. RODS AND REELS

Certainly, an angler's two most important tools.

Rods

Manufacturers produce both "spinning" and "casting" style rods in a vast array of models and sizes designed for every type of fishing imaginable. The secret is to select the exact rod, and reel, for the type of fishing planned. Freshwater trollers should have at least two, if not three, rod and reel combinations to handle all trolling needs...ultralight (4- to 6-pound test line)...medium (six- to ten-pound test line)...heavy (8- to 12-pound test line).

From a ridiculously low price to unbelievably expensive, rods are made and designed for the beginning to the discriminating professional. Do yourself a favor...test some of the higher quality rods available the next time the opportunity presents itself. Whether that moment occurs on the water using a friend's rod, or in the aisles of a sporting goods store, give it a wiggle...handle it. Better yet, if at all possible, fight a fish with it. Then make the decision.

Spinning rods and reels are called such because of the method in which line unfurls from the reel. Spinning rods are designed with larger guides at the bottom and taper in size to the smallest at the tip. The guides gradually straighten out the unfurling line, enabling anglers to cast greater distances than with level-wind models.

Many an angler has been satisfied for years with a current fishing "pole", without realizing what reduced weight and better action can do to improve enjoyment of the fight of the fish. Rods manufactured by G. Loomis, Lamiglas, Shakespeare, Fenwick and others, offer anglers state-of-the-art technological improvements for increased enjoyment and appreciation of sensitivity.

Several years ago, friends of ours fished with us at a favorite lake. The couple had recently purchased a nice, big boat and had equipped it with all the toys and whistles trollers enjoy utilizing. We were into fish and we watched our lady friend catch several fish in a row, and reel them in quite

California Inland Fisheries Foundation Chairman of the Board, Rod Browning, prefers using casting/level-wind rods and reels to subdue big trout.

proficiently. Then the rod dipped on her husband's side of the boat and because he was busy with a downrigger, he yelled for her to take the fish. She played the fish and brought it to the net, with a big smile on her face! She had just used his G. Loomis rod for the first time and it was an experience she totally enjoyed. She had been quite critical of the cost of the rod when her husband purchased it but had just realized the difference was worth it. The next time we fished together, there were four G. Loomis rods on their boat!

Reels

The quality of the reel is very important but how much to spend depends upon the angler. A high-quality reel with smooth drag systems like those produced by Penn, Shimano, Shakespeare, Pflueger and Abu-Garcia, can last a lifetime if taken care of properly. Look for reels with at least three ball bearings and sufficient spool size to hold a quantity of line in the pound test required. A spinning reel should hold at least one hundred yards of line. Most casting reels are capable of holding more than enough line. Knowing the difference between "spinning" and "casting" rods makes a big difference in matching reels to rods. Designed to suit every possible need and price range, the selections are wide and varied.

Recently, at a favorite tackle shop, we listened to the customer in line in front of us explain to the salesperson that he wanted a good rod and reel to fish for EVERYTHING from crappie to striped bass! Unfortunately, there is

Sep and Marilyn enjoy the reckless abandon and excitement of using spinning gear, even on downriggers.

Typical trolling set-up—G. Loomis CR842-2 and Calcutta 100 reels.

no rod-and-reel combo that offers great feel and action to cover all species. It is necessary for an angler to own at least a couple of combinations for fishing for multiple species of game fish.

Many anglers prefer level-wind or casting reels because they find them easier to handle and operate than spinning reels. Also, trolling with casting reels means greatly reduced line twist.

Spinning reels, often called "eggbeaters", require slightly more experience and coordination to use. Often preferred for control when fighting a fish, a spinning reel can also be an angler's worst nightmare. Reeling against the drag when fighting a fish or retrieving line can cause excessive line twist. Spinning reels come in both front and rear drag models. Performance wise, the front drag is preferred because of the larger surface area of the drag washers that allow line to move off the reel smoothly without surging or stressing it. Conversely, rear drag reels have smaller surface areas and are not as effective, especially over the long haul.

Maintain a selection of sizes of reels in both spinning and casting types. Basic rod, reel and line combinations are capable of handling fish in excess of ten pounds. The "smaller the better" works for most trolling, but there are certainly times when there is a need to match tackle to the task. The ultra-light designs create greater action…that equate to more FUN fighting fish.

After all, just like with terminal tackle…match rod and reel, to the task.

21. RAINBOW TROUT

The most planted game fish.

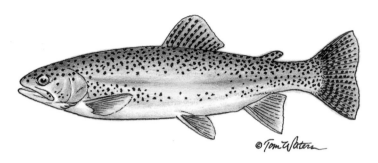

© Tom Waters

Rainbow trout are found as lake and stream trout and as anadromous or ocean migrating, stream spawning species, known as steelhead. Rainbows are second only to cutthroat in diversity of subspecies and range. Historically, that range included the Pacific Coast drainages from California to Alaska.

The leaping ability of the rainbow is what angler's dreams are made of. A hooked rainbow can leap from the water in an aerial display a dozen times or more, before reluctantly coming to the net. Rainbows readily strike offerings and can be caught on spinners, flies, grubs and a wide variety of baits ranging from nightcrawlers to minnows. Their primary diet consists mainly of insects, plankton, crustaceans, leeches, fish eggs and small minnows.

Rainbows have short heads and silver bodies with numerous small black spots along the sides. Most also display an iridescent pink stripe down the side that gives them the name "rainbow". The backs are dark green and sometimes nearly black in color. Pelvic and anal fins are tipped with white and numerous small black spots adorn the dorsal and caudal fins. Due to the diversity of conditions found in different lakes and streams, this species can display a wide variety of colors, shapes and sizes.

Growth is highly variable, depending on the habitat and available food supplies. Stream rainbows grow to about one pound in four years. However in large bodies of water where food is plentiful, rainbows can easily reach ten pounds in the same amount of time.

Classified as spring spawners, they may spawn as early as December or as late as June, depending upon the weather and elevation.

Rainbows are the most planted game fish in the Western States. They are raised in hatcheries and planted as adults and sub-adults in lakes, rivers and streams throughout the West.

22. CUTTHROAT TROUT

The distinctive streak of red on each side of the head identifies this trout.

© Tom Waters

Historically, the cutthroat had perhaps the largest range of any North American trout and the Lahontan was the largest. In the early 1900s cutts ranged from juveniles to mature fish weighing as much as 30-50 pounds and larger. Commercial fishing nearly wiped out the species and habitat loss, stream degradation and competition from non-native game fish, the rainbow trout, brown trout and mackinaw, have reduced the population and confined them to an estimated three percent of their historic range. The four recognized sub-species of cutthroat are: Coastal, West Slope, Lahontan and Yellowstone.

Cutthroat are typically light olive on the back and upper body, with silver to blush colored sides spotted with black dots. All species of cutthroat have a streak of red on each side of the lower jaw, therefore the name "cutthroat". They have larger mouths and smaller scales on the body than rainbow trout and often cross breed with rainbow trout species, which has had detrimental effects on the pure strains of cutthroat.

Depending on stream flow and water temperature, cutthroat spawn in the spring, normally from April through July. In lakes as the cutts prepare to spawn, they move in closer to shore and become easily susceptible to offerings. Cutts are often found holding near the bottom waiting for an easy meal to swim by. Strong vibrations generated by flashers and dodgers will attract cutthroat to lures, flies or properly presented grubs.

As with other species of trout, it is best to disassociate terminal tackle from boat and engine noise. Sideplaners can be used to intercept fish holding tight to shore in very shallow water and downriggers will assist in intercepting fish holding near the bottom in deeper water. Just about any type of lure is effective and the size of the lure should be appropriate for the size of the quarry. Five- to ten-pound cutts will feed on fish from two inches to twelve inches in length so an angler should be prepared with a full arsenal of lures.

23. BROWN TROUT

You don't catch big browns…you fool 'em!

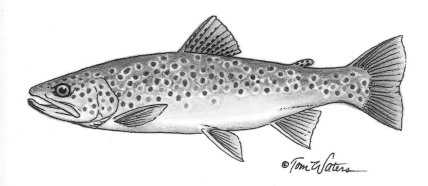

©Tom Waters

The brown trout is identified by the olive brown color with pronounced red spots surrounded by a bluish halo, found mainly on the sides of the fish from head to tail. The tail is nearly square with little or no visible spots.

Today's angler respects the brown trout because it is so difficult to catch. It is aggressive and can attain sizes of up to forty pounds, depending upon its environment and food sources. Originally, the brown was thought of as a trash fish, a moderate fighter and poor table fare. This began to change as anglers realized this hardly breed could withstand heavy fishing pressure and varied water temperatures and it tolerated pollution much better than other trout species.

Browns are elusive…they do not like sunlight, preferring dark shaded areas, dark weed growth, crevices and deep water where light penetration is greatly reduced. They are nocturnal feeders and can be found early in the morning and late in the evening, roaming shorelines in search of forage. They may be well out in the lake, following schools of kokanee or feeding on planter rainbow trout. In order for an angler to intercept a brown, you have to almost think like they do. Where will they be at a certain time of day? Natural food sources such as minnows, leeches, crayfish and insects round out their diet and primary inlets and outlets often hold browns waiting for a meal to drift by.

As tough as browns are to catch, they do drop their guard as the spawning cycle begins in the fall. As weather and water begins to cool, brown trout become more aggressive and slightly more susceptible to properly presented offerings and can often be seen rolling and swirling on the surface, chasing baitfish. Conversely, they may hold at 100 feet or more, requiring anglers to use downriggers. Spring, just after ice out, is another exceptional opportunity to catch a big brown as run-off and abundant food supplies spark the feeding instincts that were put into low gear during the cold winter months.

Big browns get big by being smart! Trolling offers anglers the best opportunity for success by covering as much water as possible and places offerings in several different aquatic environments. However, big fish are also wrestled to the net each year by surprised fishermen, working from the shoreline or anchored boats. Anglers can troll with a variety of offerings, ranging from flashers and nightcrawlers to Rapalas, trolling flies or minnow-imitating lures. Our preference is fast-trolling big lures, at one to four miles per hour, hoping for an impulse strike. The extra enticement of a small rattle in the body of a lure to increase noise and vibration can be very effective, especially in off-color or stained water conditions.

Marilyn with a 4-pound brown trout.

There exists quite a controversy about the speed to troll. Some anglers pull lures at four to six mph., others have found that a slow troll of one to two mph. is effective, especially in cold water. It is a good idea to troll offerings at 100-150 feet behind the boat when top-lining or down-rigging. Whatever choice, fast or slow, deep or shallow, it is all in the presentation. Never has the right pound test line and leader been more important! Terminal tackle and lures must be disassociated from related boat and engine noise. These fish can be spooked by anything less than natural presentation.

Don't expect to catch a trophy each time you venture out…patience and persistence will pay off in the long run! The key is luck and skill! The thrill of catching…and releasing…a monster brown trout is an exhilarating experience.

24. KOKANEE SALMON

Freshwater Sockeyes...Blue-Backs...Silver Bullets

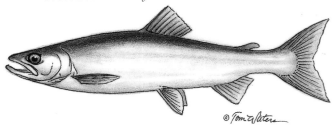

© Tom Waters

Oncorhynchus nerka is the scientific name and means "hooked nose of flowing waters". Silver in color with dotted backs and tail, most kokanee in California measure from 12-18 inches in length. Size is totally dependent upon the size of the impoundment, available nutrition and competition in the lake. Kokanee are the landlocked (non anadromous) form of sockeye salmon. They are not a trout but belong to the same family as the trout, and are found in some of the same areas. Kokanee feed almost exclusively on plankton and zooplankton.

Kokanee turn bright red during spawning periods and males produce a pronounced hooked jaw. Generally, in the fall of their third or fourth year of life, both male and female kokanee spawn and die shortly after.

For pure fight and tenacity, the kokanee is a much-respected game fish. To do battle requires specialized tackle, some skill, luck, finesse and often a great deal of patience! Often, trolling for kokanee can turn into a "Chinese fire drill". Kokanee often travel in schools, and fast hook-ups can occur at any time, followed by total inactivity until the bite starts up again.

A wide variety of specialized tactics and techniques will work on catching kokanee salmon. Trolling attractor devices such as flashers create vibrations that attract this inquisitive fish. Behind flashers, successful anglers run 14-18 inches of leader to small, brightly colored lures tipped with white corn or small pieces of nightcrawler. A rubber snubber is essential to protect leader and to keep the hook from ripping out of the kokanee's soft mouth.

For variation, small 4/0 dodgers add enticing surging, swimming action to the lures. To maximize action of the dodger, the leader to the trailing lure should be between eight and twelve inches long. Small lightweight, flutter-type lures or "bugs" work best. Some trollers even attach a set of flashers to the downrigger ball for extra fish-attracting vibration...it works!

Kokanee catching is a matter of doing EVERYTHING right and it is essential to match your tackle to the task.

25. LANDLOCKED KING SALMON

An exciting and tasty addition to any lake.

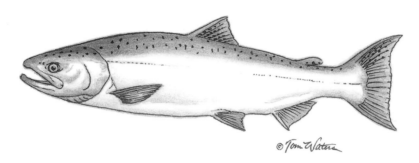

Numerous lakes and reservoirs throughout the west are planted annually with king salmon fingerlings or smolts. The addition of kings to freshwater lakes has created an additional tier for fishing, as kings occupy deeper, cooler water than most other game fish.

An exciting and tasty addition to any lake, king salmon are tireless battlers with exceptional growth rates in bodies of water where ample food supplies are available. Meat eaters that require a great deal of protein, they thrive in lakes with rich populations of pond smelt, threadfin shad or other non-game fish minnow species. They can range in size from six inches to upwards of 20 pounds plus in some lakes. A short three to four year growth period precedes the annual fall spawn.

Sep with a landlocked king salmon.

Kings are often found in schools and when one is caught, it is likely the angler will catch more if he stays with the school. Fish catching techniques are similar to those used for trout but trolling depths will be slightly deeper. Flashers and nightcrawlers or grubs work well as do dodgers and minnow-imitating lures. When using lures, tip the hook with a piece of nightcrawler to increase odds of success. Rapalas, smeared with scent, work underwater wonders when trolled as fast as two to three miles per hour.

26. MACKINAW

Also called lake trout

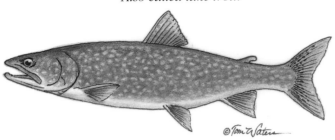

Mackinaw, also known as lake trout, are actually a member of the char family. They are generally found in deep, cold waters that often hold populations of rainbow trout, brown trout and kokanee salmon. Mainly a forage fish, they feed heavily on small baitfish, planter trout or non-game fish species like squawfish, suckers, smelt or sculpins. In some lakes, out of necessity, they feed almost exclusively on plankton, insects or crustaceans. "Macks" require cold, well-oxygenated water and in summer often move to depths of 50 to 100 feet, and deeper. In spring and fall, they can be found at depths of 20 feet or less in many lakes. Their preferred water temperature range is from 40 to 52 degrees.

Lake trout are slow growing, especially in very cold water environments but are a long-lived specie, sometimes reaching an age of 40 years. In cold-water climates, where "thaw-out" may last only 100 days, it may take 15 years for a "laker" to reach two pounds. Most macks are caught in the two to 20-pound range but in many Western states, will often grow in excess of 30 pounds or more.

The lake trout is green to olive in color and has spots and marbling distributed on fins, tail and sides and to some extent, on its unique forked tail.

Fishing for mackinaw requires specialized tackle and techniques. A high-quality locator capable of deepwater readings, is essential. Downriggers are important and depending upon depths where the macks are hanging, it may be necessary to use wire line. Terminal gear varies greatly from pearl Kwik-fish and J-Plugs to dodgers and threaded minnow set-ups, where legal. Minnow-imitating lures such as Rapalas and Apex in rainbow, pearl or kokanee color patterns can also be trolled effectively behind flashers or dodgers.

Lake trout wage strong, determined underwater battles, fighting, as many guides say, with their "shoulders" with short forceful runs and give-and-take pulls. Most are taken by trolling with spoons or minnow-imitating lures attached to wire line or downriggers.

27. STATE-OF-THE-ART TECHNOLOGY

A mix of electronics and technology gives the angler tools to consistently catch fish.

Sorting through the array of available trolling tools is like wandering through a maze of gadgets and gimmicks designed to catch as many fishermen as fish. New technology and ideas bring additional products to the retail market every year. There are many new tools that anglers can use to improve their fishing, the quality of their fishing, and most important, the enjoyment of that fishing.

Nautamatic TR1

The single-most important tool to aid trollers is made by Nautamatic Marine Systems. The TR-1 is an automatic pilot steering system designed for trolling motors from six to twenty-five horsepower. It operates from a computer-based electrohydraulic system, a hand-held remote control, flux-gate compass and a sophisticated gyro. This advanced technological device automatically makes directional changes for the slightest variations caused by wind, waves or cur-rents. It has changed the way anglers fish by offering a most convenient hands-free operation, making it much simpler to set downriggers, test temperatures, net fish and re-rig, without having to constantly hold on and steer with the tiller.

We have nicknamed ours the "Marriage Saver"…no more over-steering, no more drifting off course, no more tense comments! It is easy to set the direction with the control device and the boat simply stays on course, hands free. We troll along calmly with minimum effort. Technology at work!

Computrol Products

Computrol, parent company of Cannon downriggers and BottomLine locators continues to be on the cutting edge of technology with several trolling products. Sidefinder fish locators, downriggers and sideplaners combine into what Cannon calls its Down and Out total trolling system.

Cannon Electric Mini Mag, Mag 10, Mag 20 and Digi-Troll Downriggers

Want to keep down-rigged lures or bait at a certain distance above the bottom of the lake? A downrigger is a must! The Cannon Digi-Troll downrigger will raise and lower lures or bait at certain intervals. A sensitive, bottom-following mode lets it track the bottom contour, keeping offerings at a preset distance. The cycle function raises and lowers the depth of the downrigger ball at predetermined depths and time intervals to add a jigging action to lures or bait.

Computrol is proud of the fact that Cannon electric downriggers were the first to incorporate Positive Ion Control into each unit. P.I.C. charges the downrigger cable with a metered, low-voltage, fish-attracting electrical current. The relatively small electrical field created by the voltage attracts fish to the downriggers. The positive voltage adjusts between .6 and 1.2 volts, perfect for attracting rather than repelling fish. The benefits of the fish-attracting positive currents have been extolled for years by commercial fishermen. This technology has now been passed on to anglers who want a simple, built-in, easy to use unit.

BottomLine NCC6500 Navigation Command Center with Sidefinder Capabilities

Computrol has taken another leap forward in technology with the introduction of this fish locator. The unit gives big-screen viewing in five directions simultaneously. It is now possible to find fish up to 240 feet to the sides of the boat and still have the capacity to look 1,500 feet down. In terms of water volume searched, the standard twenty-

degree cone on most competitive units scans less than 1,000 cubic feet of water. The Sidefinder technology increases the visual locating zone to over four million cubic feet of water. The split screen feature lets the angler customize the screen to include a graph, flasher, five-way viewer and an optional GPS or Loran system.

Cannon Dual Plane-R-Board

To further enhance fishing and truly make the Cannon "Down and Out" system complete, Sidefinder technology can be matched with the Dual Plane-R-Board devices that allow anglers to troll to both sides of the boat, up to 150 feet away. This creates a unique system that enables the angler to not only see fish on the screen, but to present lures to those fish holding or moving to the sides. Acting much like outriggers, they enable a troller to run several lines out to each side at varying distances away from the boat.

Cannon Speed-and-Temp

Cannon produces a unit known as the Speed-and-Temp that knowledgeable anglers have been using for years. A transducer attached just above the downrigger ball transmits a radio signal to the locator. It gives a digital read-out indicating trolling speed, surface temperature, temperature at the downrigger ball, and the percentage of available light intensity at the downrigger ball. The unit constantly relays information that indicates to the angler the depth to fish (thermocline temperature), color of lure to use (based on depth and light), and trolling speed (based on water temperature at the lure).

GPS/C-MAP – Locators and Hand-Held Units

An ever-growing number of anglers have learned the benefits of Global Positioning System...GPS...navigational receivers. Whether dash-mounted on your boat and tied into your locator, or hand-held portable units, the GPS has become an important tool for both tournament and recreational anglers alike.

Anglers who find prime fishing spots such as drop-offs, reefs, humps and springs, can permanently and accurately record that location in the GPS unit memory. This enables an angler to return to the exact spot to intercept feeding fish at that same location, time after time. These units are so accurate that some anglers now scout lakes by airplane and store the way-point settings of prime fish-holding locations.

Underwater Cameras

Technology continues to amaze us; the ability to clearly view in deep water, on a monitor, what is underneath the boat, or follow a down-rigged offering, and to record the information for future viewing, is a major step forward. An angler can distinguish actual fish and watch the action of the lure, see the fish move toward it, then the hit and the fight. Small waterproof units, in black and white, infra-red or color, come with rechargeable batteries, making it possible to have this technology available and useable right in the boat.

Minn Kota Electric Trolling Motor

Minn Kota leads the way in product innovations and cutting-edge technology. The Power Drive Motor, equipped with the auto pilot feature, makes steering in windy conditions and choppy water much easier, regardless of wind, waves or current. The angler can set direction and trolling speed and utilize the "hands free" operation to change lures, set downriggers, fight a fish or simply enjoy the scenery.

The new Co-Pilot feature—a wireless system designed specifically to work with Minn Kota electric motors—features a small remote control, similar to an automobile keyless entry, that can take full command of the steering, speed control and on-off operation from anywhere in the boat. It can be worn around the neck, on a belt, on the wrist or attached to a rod while fishing.

A Dual Pro electric charger finishes off the system. By simply plugging in an extension cord, all on-board batteries can be charged in six hours or less. Never has trolling been easier and Minn Kota makes it happen!

We can be assured that technology will continue to provide anglers with bigger and better "toys". There is no end to what can be imagined, dreamed, invented or built and anglers will always look for new and innovative products in their quest for assistance in locating and catching their quarry.

28. "GET A CLUE!"

Poaching fish

Most noticeable everywhere is that many fishermen put their "keep-ers" on stringers, and then dangle them over the side of the boat. In cool fall and winter conditions, this is probably an adequate way of keeping fish fresh. However, in bright sunlight and very warm temperatures, it probably will not take long to "poach" the catch.

If planning to keep fish, it is always best to dispatch…kill…them immediately. As fish struggle and die on stringers or flop in empty ice chests or drained live wells, they build up lactic acid that begins to break down the muscles. The meat gets mushy, quickly. A swift "bonk" on the head…a quick "wood shampoo", is the fastest way to dispatch the catch. Put the fish immediately on ice and keep it cold. This will slow the natural breakdown of the meat and will keep it fresher and firmer. The difference will definitely be noticed.

Next time you go fishing and plan to keep some fish, take along plenty of ice.

Releasing Fish

If you want to "catch and release"…once you have that fish to the boat, you need to react quickly. The fish is tired and stressed after the fight, and if you want photos, keep that camera handy and ready to shoot. You have about as much time as you can hold your breath to get the photo and unhook the fish. That's about a minute, which is plenty if you are prepared…not very long, if you have to fumble around. Keep your equipment close at hand.

What can you do to help a fish survive? Keep it in the water and try not to wipe off the protective slime that will help keep the fish alive. Wet your hands and hold the fish just behind its head, right over its gill covers. Do not touch its gills or eyes and do not squeeze its stomach.

Pulling on the hook just sinks it in deeper. Grab the eye of the hook and try to push it back into the fish's mouth. Once the barbed end is free, slide the hook out. Needlenose pliers definitely help. If the lifesaving technique appears to be failing, do not waste the fish, keep it.

Launching Your Boat

Launching a boat on a ramp requires practice. To learn, first take your boat and trailer to an empty parking lot, so you don't practice on a busy launch ramp.

When backing down the ramp, the trailer turns in the direction opposite to the direction you turn the steering wheel. To adjust for this, place your hand on the bottom of the steering wheel. Now, when you turn the wheel to the right, the trailer will turn to the right. Roll down the window and watch what is going on.

Before backing down the ramp, pull over to the side of the road in the designated area, to take off the boat cover, remove tie downs, unplug the lights, load coolers and fishing gear, and make sure every passenger has a US Coast Guard approved life jacket ready to wear.

One more thing—be very sure you have placed the drain plug into the boat!

Launch Ramp Courtesy

Time on the ramp should be very limited, which means, be ready. Be efficient, prompt and thoughtful. All the guys lined up behind you are anxious to get into the water too. Your turn comes up when your vehicle is next in line, proceeding to the ramp, whether you are launching, or taking your boat off the water.

Do every bit of preparation before backing your vehicle down. There is nothing worse than waiting behind guys placing electric motors, batteries, dogs, kids, coolers, or whatever, into the boat...on the launch ramp.

In the dark, turn headlights OFF on your vehicle so the next guy lining up isn't totally disoriented in the glare of lights. You cannot see to back up when you've got headlights in your rear-view mirror.

Once launched, get your boat moved as far along the docks as possible, making room for others behind. Get your vehicle parked correctly, in an assigned space, and hurry back to your boat. Get it started...and get out of the way.

Be aware of the surroundings...think about what you are doing...and instead of creating ramp rage, your efforts will be appreciated.

Be a Good Sport

Know the rules and regulations and practice courtesy and safety. Troll far enough away from anchored or stillfishing anglers to give them room to cast. If anchored, leave enough room between boats to allow trollers to motor through. Courtesy dictates that you should keep at least a 30- to 50-yard buffer zone to avoid crossing over or tangling lines with fellow anglers. Be particularly careful about wakes when passing through anchored boats. Go slow!

PLEASE don't follow another troller too closely. Avoid crossing too close to the bow of another boater...you're just asking for trouble. Always envision where your lure is. If you drag your line and lure in front of another troller's boat, chances are you'll get into his line or downriggers. Be observant…pay attention to what is happening…in your boat and in the water around you…think about what you're doing and get into the rhythm, or pathway of the others around you.

Exhibiting common sense and common courtesy will make your adventures far more enjoyable.

Boating Safety

Most boating fatalities each year involve fishermen and almost all of these could have been avoided if people would pay attention to a few boating safety issues.

All folks in the boat should wear a lifejacket. Many styles are available, most of them not bulky or uncomfortable and for safety's sake, should be worn at all times. Count the people you take with you and do not go over the limitations of the boat. Keep everyone seated and if one person has to stand up to fight a fish, make sure others do not rock the boat. Passengers should not block your view—be aware of what is ahead, especially until the boat planes out and you can see in front.

Drive your boat at a safe speed. Slow down to make turns and don't create hazardous wakes and be careful crossing other boater's wakes. Be extra cautious around dams, bridges or in unfamiliar waters.

Last, but not least, boating and alcohol do not mix!

Dress for the Season

It may be warm where you are, but if your trip will take you into higher elevations, temperatures become considerably colder, the higher up you go. Every 100 feet of elevation decreases degrees. If you don't plan ahead, you can end up very cold and uncomfortable. For one thing, bring the boat top and zip-in windows, if you have them.

Take along plenty of warm clothing. It is a good idea to dress in layers. Take long underwear, a shirt and jacket and raingear. You will need good boots and socks, a hat and gloves. If the weather cooperates and the sun shines, start peeling. At that point, you will need sunglasses and sunblock.

Often conditions are totally unpredictable, no matter what time of year, or what the forecasters say. A fishing opportunity is precious time on the water and if you're wet and cold, or frying in the sun, it becomes something you want to cut short, instead of enjoying every moment.

Don't Get Lost

Weather conditions change quickly during fall and winter months and if you're participating in outdoor activities, you can't afford to get lost…out in the wilderness, or on the water.

"GET A CLUE!"

Know where you are at all times and the best way to do this involves using a map and compass. Never leave home without these tools, be familiar with them, and keep them handy. Your sense of direction isn't nearly as dependable as a compass, so constantly look for landmarks and look behind you as well as in front. Pay attention to everything around you!

State-of-the-art technology has brought us the hand-held Global Positioning System, or GPS, the most important navigational aid ever. It truly is a great tool. However, when night falls or reception weakens or batteries die, you can end up in trouble.

Tell other people where you are going and always be prepared. Have heavy clothing and extra food along...plus the cell phone...in case you do get off the beaten track.

Never take chances...it's just not worth it!

Carbon Monoxide

Whatever type of fishing you do, be well prepared for the elements. When weather patterns are not stabilized, you could start out with sunshine in the morning, and by mid-afternoon find yourself in the midst of a major storm.

If your boat has windows and doors that can be zipped in at a moments notice, this helps. Just one thing though, make very sure you have adequate ventilation inside that warm cocoon. Carbon monoxide is a silent killer, creeping in undetected. The exhaust from an outboard engine can quickly fill the enclosed space on your boat and it WILL asphyxiate and kill you.

Carbon monoxide is colorless, odorless, tasteless and non-irritating and unless you use a CO detector, you don't even notice its presence. It can cause headache, nausea, weakness and dizziness and in some cases, is written off as seasickness. By the time you realize there is a problem, you may be too weak to open a door or move outside to fresh air. You have to have ventilation...it might save your life!

Spring Motors

If your boat and motor spend the winter in the garage, it's a good idea to start the season off with a spring "check-up".

Modern motors are assembled with exact tolerances, and nuts and bolts are pulled up to precise torque settings, so it's smart to leave the major overhauls to the professionals. However, if you think you can do the tune-up or some part of it yourself, go for it in the comfort of home, rather than on the side of the road.

Check fuel line for obstructions and leaks—remove, clean and re-gap spark plugs, or start off with new plugs—check wiring and replace any that's cracked, worn or dried out—remove propeller and check the shear pin, and ensure the impeller is working—use the right oil and good grade of regular gasoline—and don't mess with the fuel ratio recommended by the manufacturer. Start off with fun...instead of frustration!

Winter Motors

If you're on a fishing trip in a high-elevation location and temperatures drop at night, take care of your boat motor, or motors. Before you tuck yourself in for the night, tuck your motors in too. Cover them with a blanket or tarp to keep away the cold and protect them from frost. They will start easier.

When you finish your day's fishing and put your boat back on the trailer, be sure to drain all the water out of the engines. When you lower them for the night, be sure all the water is drained, or you could have a problem the next morning. While you stay warm at night, make sure the engines are comfortable too!

Trailer Bearings

If you tow your boat on its trailer everywhere...on country roads, on highways, on gravel and dusty roads...check wheel bearings and hubs regularly and often. It's a good idea to check the bearings thoroughly one year, and replace them every other year.

Keep bearings full, not overloaded, with good marine-grade grease. Carry an extra set, just in case, plus the tools you might need, including a grease gun.

Visually inspect trailer wheels and tires and check the air pressure. Tighten lug nuts and the trailer hitch ball, plus make sure the winch is working smoothly. One bad experience and you will definitely be prepared to handle boat-trailer emergencies in the future.

Road Rules

When towing your boat on the freeway, the maximum speed allowed is 55 miles per hour. The other known fact is that you're to tow your boat in the right hand or slow lane only.

If you need to pass a slower vehicle in the slow lane, the law allows you to move left over one lane, make your move, then return to the slow lane.

If you're traveling on three lanes, you may move into the middle lane to pass, then back to the slow lane. When on a four-lane freeway, you may travel on either of the two right lanes, only. The law does not allow you to pass in either of the two left lanes. If you do it and get caught, be ready to pay a healthy fine.

Read the Instructions

Got a new locator, new downriggers, some far-out tackle, or accessories, or rod and reel? Have you tried to use something and it just didn't work...until someone suggested you READ and follow the instructions!

Manufacturers give directions, drawings and often even videos to help you use their products to maximum potential. The only way you'll get the most out of any item is to know how it works, and that applies to something as simple as a lure, or as complex as electronic locators.

Look at the packaging, read the back side before you toss it in the garbage. Or, read the instruction booklet, BEFORE, not after, using the new item. And keep that information around to refresh your mind a couple of months from now. Save yourself a lot of frustration!

Tipping Your Guide

If you've gone fishing with a guide lately and you were treated well, hopefully you tipped your guide appropriately. Tipping is an accepted practice, following are some guidelines that will help you make a good decision.

For an AVERAGE, decent trip, a nice experience, using good equipment, and your guide has good basic knowledge, tip ten percent. Two guys out on a $300 deal would tip $30, or $15 each.

A GOOD trip, with a guide having decent knowledge, who knows more than you do and cares about his extra nice boat and equipment, would warrant a tip of 15 to 20 percent. That $300 trip would tip around $50.

A GREAT day, an excellent time, a cream-of-the-crop trip, with a professional guide with good personality and ability to show you he knows what he's talking about, who provides top-notch equipment and gives results no matter what, justifies a 25 percent tip. On a $300 deal, that's $75 to $100.

Choose trips carefully...make your time out on the water one that provides good memories—and tip accordingly.

Protect Your Belongings

Most folks you meet in the Great Outdoors are nice, honest, dependable, right? Well, maybe not everybody fits that description. Don't get burned by burglars!

Protect vehicles, boats and belongings by taking precautions when you leave them in remote areas, or even in launch ramp parking. Never leave stuff in plain view of passersby. Hide gear in the trunk, under the seats or cover with clothes. Roll up windows and always lock vehicles and campers. Use good locks on boat engines and boat trailers. An alarm is a practical addition and even out in the boonies, the shriek will send most burglars running.

Keep track of fishing rods and tackle boxes and do not leave them in tempting locations. Trust no one...not everybody is a nice guy!

Cigarette Butts

Anglers who smoke are intelligent, caring, knowledgeable people who refuse to believe the scary news we're exposed to daily. We tolerate your obnoxious habit, but....

Butts, as in cigarettes and cigars, do not mix well with water. When you casually toss your leftover butt into the lake or stream, keep in mind that it will not dissolve and chances are some fish will come along and slurp it up. Butts do not digest in the stomach, so the fish will die.

So what's the answer? A good friend of ours smokes his cigarettes down-wind of everyone, he carries a small metal container with cover in his pocket, and he places his cigarette butts into it. The butts don't go in the water and there is no smell on board the boat. What a guy! He knows his habit is offensive and says, "Butts are like opinions...everyone's got one and most of them stink"!

Keep it Clean

On a recent fishing trip, we trolled into a long scenic arm of a lake. Trees hung over the water, creating cool shady spots, there were birds on the shoreline and we marveled at the vegetation and ferns. We saw no other boats and were enjoying the isolation of this pristine area...pristine?

In many places along the shoreline, glistening in the afternoon sun, was garbage—beer and soda cans, glass bottles, paper wrappers, Styrofoam cups and nightcrawler containers, plus much more unidentifiable debris. On the launch ramp area, we had to watch where we walked as there was so much broken glass in the rocks and sand. How sad that people think so little of our environment.

Don't be a thoughtless litterer. When you leave, there should be no sign you've been there! Pick it up, pack it home, dispose of it properly and do your bit to make this world one we can all enjoy.

"GET A CLUE!"

Check out what we do...

SEP'S PRO FISHING, INC. manufactures ultralight trolling products.

Designed by Sep and Marilyn Hendrickson, SEP'S line of trolling products...

Pro Flashers, Mini Micro Flashers, Pro Dodgers, Side Kick Dodgers, Pro Secret Lures, Kokanee Kandy Lures, Pro Trolling Flies, Sure Release and Sure Stacker, Pro SidePlaner—all intended for light line use.

Check out: www.seps.com for complete details.

Sep's on the Radio

Sep is the host of "California Sportsmen", an award-winning weekly radio show, broadcast on Saturday mornings from 6:00 to 8:00AM on KHTK 1140 AM, Sacrament. This popular show offers the most current information on fishing Northern California's lakes, streams, rivers, bay and ocean and is designed to keep anglers informed about what's going on in their favorite locales. But, it's not just a "fishing show", it's much more.

Sep takes you live on the water, "Virtual Fishing" all over the Western States, His "on the Scene" interviews with professional fishing guides and experts provide listeners with acquired expertise and knowledge on the water. The "on Location" segments take place in the blind or in the field, hunting for birds or deer and pigs, and "Destinations" provides details on travel and vacation opportunities. In addition, interviews with top outdoor writers, Department of Fish and Game personnel, prominent magazine editors, resort owners and other well-known fishing and hunting personalities keep listeners up-to-speed on great outdoor action.

California Sportsmen—bringing the best in outdoor entertainment!

IN CLOSING

We enjoy what we do!

As all anglers know, catching fish remains a matter of being in the right place at the right time, at the right depth, at the right speed, with the right lure, in the right color, with the correct action and proper presentation. As technology continues to improve, taking advantage of what is available will certainly help anglers catch more fish. We need all the help we can get and we know that good equipment plus good luck equals good fishing!

There are times when looking at at fish becomes an almost religious experience!

The main thing is to get out there and do it! No matter how successful the angler, the privilege of being in our great outdoors is in itself a reward…AND A FISH IN THE NET IS A FINE BONUS.

Take care of our resource by keeping only what is needed…release the rest to grow and provide anticipation and excitement for anglers to come.

Practice C.P.R., "catch, photograph and release"! There are times that looking at that fish in the net becomes an almost religious experience. Having a photograph can bring back a happy memory!

We are so glad to be a part of this wonderful sport of FISHING!

MORE BOOKS FOR FISHERMEN

EGG CURES: PROVEN RECIPES & TECHNIQUES

SCOTT HAUGEN

Of all the natural baits, many consider eggs to be the best. Scott Haugen has gone to the experts—fishermen and fishing guides—to get their favorite egg cures and fishing techniques, plus their secret tricks and tips. The result is this book. These 28 recipes come from anglers who catch fish—read this book and you will too. Guaranteed! 5 1/2 × 8 1/2 inches, 90 pages.

SB: $15.00   ISBN: 1-57188-238-3

WHAT FISH SEE
DR. COLIN KAGEYAMA, O.D.

An in-depth examination by Dr. Colin Kageyama of how and what fish see. This important book will help all anglers to design better flies and lures by its explanation of the physical processes of light in water and consequently how colors change and are perceived by fish in varying conditions of depth, turbidity, and light. Excellent illustrations by Vic Erickson and color plates that show startling color changes. This book will change the way you fish! 6 × 9 inches, 184 pages.

SB: $19.95   ISBN: 1-57188-140-9

TYING STRONG FISHING KNOTS

BILL HERZOG

We have all had a knot break or come undone on a big fish. Use this extremely helpful book to tie excellent knots. Crisp, easy-to-understand illustrations and text show you how to tie all the general and specialized fishing knots you'll ever need, as well as fly fishing knots. This is a handy book to keep in your tackle box. 5 1/2 × 8 1/2 inches, 48 pages.

SB: $6.95   ISBN: 1-57188-022-4

HOW FISH WORK
DR. TOM SHOLSETH

Sholseth discusses: what is "scientific angling"?; angler characteristics; the aquatic environment in which they fish; equipment; effect of different kinds of light on fish; their senses and behaviors; the predator/prey relationship; strike responses; handling fish; creating a field guide; how the placement of your lure or fly looks to the fish; how to design more effective fly patterns; everything you need to understand and appreciate the species for which you fish. 8 1/2 × 11, inches, 80 pages.

SB: $19.95   ISBN: 1-57188-239-1

ROD-BUILDING GUIDE
FLY, SPINNING, CASTING, TROLLING
TOM KIRKMAN

Building your own rod is challenging, rewarding, and fun! Tom covers: blanks and components; rod-building tools; adhesive and bonding techniques; understanding rod spine; grip, handle, and seat assembly; guide placement, guide prep and wrapping; finishing; and more. For the beginner and from which an old pro can learn some new techniques. Full color, 8 1/2 × 11 inches, 51 pages.

SB: $14.95   ISBN: 1-57188-216-2

KOKANEE
A COMPLETE FISHING GUIDE
DAVE BISER

Kokanee salmon are found throughout North America. These chunky, tasty lake-dwelling salmon are challenging to catch unless you know the special techniques. Biser reveals all the techniques and various sorts of terminal tackle, baits, and lures. This is the first in-depth book about this wonderful national game fish, 5 1/2 × 8 1/2 inches, 180 pages.

SB: $14.95   ISBN: 1-57188-120-4

Ask for these books at your local fishing or book store or order from:
1-800-541-9498 (8 to 5 p.s.t.) • www.amatobooks.com
Frank Amato Publications, Inc. • P.O. Box 82112 • Portland, Oregon 97282